A Schoolman in

THE LAW LI[illegible]

Problems

Bibliography

Research Tools

Analysis of a Case

Glossary of Legal Terms

by

ARTHUR A. REZNY, Ph.D.
Associate Professor of Education
The University of Wisconsin-Milwaukee

Second Edition

Danville, Illinois: THE INTERSTATE Printers & Publishers, Inc.

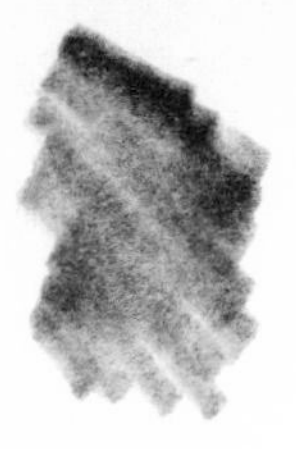

First Edition, 1962

PRINTED IN U.S.A.

TO

Madaline Kinter Remmlein, Ph.D., J.D.
Author, Lecturer, and Founder of the National Organization
of Legal Problems in Education (NOLPE)

It is with deep regret that this second edition of *A Schoolman in the Law Library* is published without the original co-author. It is hoped that during her years of retirement and in the future we will not forget her contributions to the area of legal problems in education.

TABLE OF CONTENTS

INTRODUCTION

This booklet has been prepared to describe law books and their use by schoolmen, primarily graduate students of education. These school-law research sources are not only explained and illustrated; opportunity for practice in their use is provided through numerous exercises.

The problems in the exercises are intended to introduce the student in education, and in particular in school administration, to some of the main classes of legal materials with which he will be dealing during a course in school law. By finding the answers to the questions, the student should gain some familiarity with the method used for seeking legal information. It is not expected that he will learn any law or basic principles by answering the questions, nor is it expected that all phases of the use of the law library will be mastered. It is assumed that some explanation of the use of the law library and study of Chapter I of this booklet have preceded an attempt to answer the questions.

Because of the importance of case law in a school-law course, students should be able to "analyze a case" so as to summarize the essential facts, define the major issues in dispute, and deduce the legal principles on which the decision was based. Since this type of study is not ordinarily used in education courses, other than in school law, a sample "ANALYSIS OF A CASE" is included in this booklet. It may serve as a guide, though not necessarily is it held up by the authors as a perfect model from which there should be no deviations.

The "GLOSSARY OF LEGAL TERMS," a substitute for a law dictionary, will aid the student in understanding language used by legislators and judges by giving him a quick and handy reference. At times, it will be necessary to refer to a law dictionary.

The "BIBLIOGRAPHY" serves the dual purpose of referring the student to the latest treatises and miscellaneous references, and by including old references for research purposes, of making the student aware of the fact that the field of school law has been of interest to educators and to some attorneys for many years. Most publications which are limited to a particular state are not included. New treatises and articles appear in print at frequent intervals. Such materials can be located in the *Public Catalog*, *Education Index*, and the *Index to Legal Periodicals*. The Bibliography serves as a point of departure.

Through an understanding of the use of the law library, the student will save much time in preparing a paper on subjects of his special interest and will be able to conduct a more thorough and professional project. This booklet may prove helpful for future professional activities when the days of graduate study have long since past.

A.A.R.

Chapter I

LEGAL RESEARCH TOOLS AND HOW TO USE THEM*

In the following pages directions will be given for legal research on school-law topics, particularly those included in this text, by use of legal research tools. Descriptions of these tools must, of necessity, be brief; photostatic copies of pages from some of the law books serve as illustrations. However, only by actually working with these devices can their real value be learned.

Constitutions

The Federal Constitution and the constitution of the particular state are usually placed at the beginning of each state code of general laws. The Federal Constitution appears in the United States Code also.

Some editions of these constitutions are annotated; others are not. An index to the constitutional provisions may be included in the index to statutory provisions, or a separate index to each constitution may be given.

Although it is occasionally possible to obtain a compilation in one volume of constitutional provisions of all states, these compilations go out of date; and, aside from the undesirability of using a secondary source, it is safer to use the state constitution included in each of the latest state code of laws, because this copy will contain all amendments to date.

State Statutes

Almost every state department of education publishes from time to time a compilation of state laws relating to education. Some of these publications appear infrequently and are difficult to use without further search for later enactments. Supplements may be issued be-

* Adapted from *School Law* by Madaline Kinter Remmlein, Danville, Ill.: The Interstate Printers & Publishers, Inc., 1962.

tween dates of complete compilations, but search through a half dozen or more pamphlets is a tedious task and one which is subject to error unless done very carefully.

There is a more serious objection to using some state department publications. These compilations of state school laws in some states are arranged in a sequence and numbered differently from the arrangement used in the state code of general laws for the particular state. This practice was more general a few years ago than at present. It is undesirable because, when the state department issues the school law codified according to its own departmental numerical plan, legal research tools applicable to the codification of the official state code cannot be used.

However, a number of state departments now publish the school laws using the codification of the official state code. In such cases, section 1198, for example, in the state department publication is identical with section 1198 of the state code of general laws. Then the devices of legal research may be used as easily with the state department publication as with the state code, provided it is not too far out of date for use as a point of departure. Some state department publications use both their own and the official codification numbers to identify each section, in which case the state department numbers can be ignored in legal research.

One point in favor of using state department publications on school law is their availability to educators. However, warning should be made that before any such bulletin is used it should be examined to ascertain its codification plan. Usually the preface explains the numbering system of the bulletin.

In view of the variation in usability among state department publications of school laws, it is recommended that state codes of general laws be used wherever available, either instead of the state department publication or in connection with it. State codes are more frequently published in practically every state, and are usually kept currently up to date by cumulative supplements or pocket parts; they are more completely indexed usually; they are arranged and numbered in a way which allows the use of legal research tools to be described later.

Some states recompile general statutes after each legislative session (usually every odd year). Those with pocket parts do not issue new compilations until the pocket parts become too bulky to be included in the cover of the publication. A few states have neither pocket parts nor frequent recompilations, but these instances are rare.

The publications having pocket parts are especially useful. In the back cover of each of these volumes is a pocket in which is inserted at frequent intervals the new laws and amendments to the statutes included in the bound part of the volume, coordinated into the codification scheme. If the edition is annotated, the pocket part includes annotations to cases which have interpreted the statutes in the bound part of the volume, as well as any statutory changes, the sections being identified by their numbers. Thus, the pocket parts keep the compilation up to date.

For enactments later than the latest code, supplement, or pocket part, session laws must be used. In most states, only the last session need be cited to session laws, since pocket parts, or supplements, or revisions of the entire code bring the statutes up to within a year or two of any given date.

Most compilations of general statutes are annotated. Volumes which are annotated contain, commonly under each section of the law, the history of the statute or the section and citations to court cases in which it has been mentioned.

Exhibit 1 shows a copy of page 148 from the *Annotated Code of Maryland*. The page number is at the bottom of the page. However, page numbers are not usually used in statute citations. For example, if one were referring to the Maryland law on suspension and expulsion of pupils, the citation would be to section 131, not to page 148. At the top of the page it may be seen that sections 130-133 are shown on this page.

The school laws of Maryland are compiled in Article 77. The Maryland Code uses "articles" for main headings which are on the level called "titles" in most statutory compilations.

At the end of each section, in parentheses, are citations to former codes containing identical or similar provisions. This is the "legislative history" of the section. Almost all statutory compilations include legislative history even though other types of annotations may not be included. The Maryland Code does include other types of annotations: cross references and citations to court decisions in which each section has been interpreted. The value of statutory annotations can be seen easily from this example. Although, of course, different states follow different styles, the Maryland Code is typical.

participation as if they were teachers employed in the public schools, subject to all the conditions, limitations and restrictions imposed by § 127 of this article. (An. Code, 1951, § 123; 1939, § 110; 1939, ch. 399.)

CHAPTER 9. PUPILS

§ 130. Admission.

All white youths between the ages of six and twenty-one years shall be admitted into such public schools of the State, the studies of which they may be able to pursue; provided, that whenever there are grade schools, the principal and the county superintendent shall determine to which school pupils shall be admitted. (An. Code, 1951, § 124; 1939, § 111; 1924, § 114; 1912, § 63; 1904, § 59; 1888, § 54; 1872, ch. 377; 1916, ch. 506, § 63.)

Cross reference.—See note to § 1 of this article.

The effect of the decision in Brown v. Board of Education, 347 U. S. 483, 74 S. Ct. 686, 98 L. Ed. 873, was to strike the word "white" out of this section. Robinson v. Board of Education, 143 F. Supp. 481.

Individual Negro children now have the right to apply under this section for admission to a particular school, and from the decision of the county superintendent on such application an appeal lies to the State Board. Whether the refusal of such an application would also give an immediate right to file proceedings in a State court to determine any question of law involved, or to file proceedings in this court to review any alleged deprivation of constitutional rights, might depend upon the reason or reasons for such refusal. Robinson v. Board of Education, 143 F. Supp. 481.

And when denied admission have an adequate administrative remedy.—Colored children denied admission to the school of their choice have an adequate administrative remedy by way of application to the county superintendent for admission, and appeal to the State Board from any decision of the county superintendent adverse to their application. Robinson v. Board of Education, 143 F. Supp. 481.

Formerly, separation of races was valid where equal facilities provided.—See Williams v. Zimmerman, 172 Md. 563, 192 A. 353.

Cited in Boyer v. Garrett, 88 F. Supp. 353, aff'd in 183 F. (2d) 582.

§ 131. Suspension and explusion.

The district board of school trustees shall have power, to suspend and expel pupils for cause; provided, that an appeal shall be to the county superintendent, whose decision shall be final. (An. Code, 1951, § 125; 1939, § 112; 1924, § 115; 1912, § 64; 1904, § 60; 1888, § 55; 1872, ch. 377; 1916, ch. 506, § 64.)

§ 132. Attendance in adjoining district.

Children living remote from the school of the district in which they reside may attend school in an adjoining district, with the consent of the county superintendent of schools. (An. Code, 1951, § 126; 1939, § 113; 1924, § 116; 1912, § 65; 1904, § 61; 1888, § 56; 1872, ch. 377; 1916, ch. 506, § 65.)

§ 133. Vaccination.

Every child before being admitted to any public school shall produce a certificate from a regular physician that he has been properly vaccinated. (An. Code, 1951, § 127; 1939, § 114; 1924, § 117; 1912, § 66; 1904, § 62; 1888, § 57; 1872, ch. 377.)

Cross references.—See § 134 et seq. As to State vaccine agency, see article 43, § 68 et seq. As to duties of teachers relative to vaccination of pupils, see article 43, § 74.

148

Exhibit 1. Photostatic copy of page 148 in Volume 7 of the *Annotated Code of Maryland*. Reproduced with permission of the publisher and copyright owner, The Michie Company, Charlottesville, Va.

Shepard's Citations to Statutes. To find out what has happened to a statute since the date of the official state code publication, one turns to Shepard's Citations to Statutes. To find cases more recent than those included in the annotated statutes, or those for any reason omitted from the annotations, if any, or in a state where the code is not annotated, the same citator is used. With one or two exceptions, every state is covered by this periodical device for finding changes in laws and citations to cases where the statute has been mentioned by a court in connection with particular facts. By using Shepard's Citations to Statutes one may discover every instance where any particular section of any law has been affected by subsequent legislation and every instance where it has been cited, applied, or construed by the courts.

The method used in these citators is merely the listing of the section numbers of the statutes with reference to the later enactments and the court decisions, each preceded by an abbreviation which tells the story of what happened in each instance. These abbreviations[1] cover many situations, a few of which are listed herewith:

A (amended) means that the statute was amended.

Ad (added) means that a new section was added without affecting the numbering of the old section.

R (rejected or repealed) means that an existing statute has been abrogated.

S (superseded) means that new legislation was substituted for an existing statute but the old statute was not expressly abrogated.

U (unconstitutional) means that the court has declared the statute unconstitutional.

C (constitutional) means that the court has upheld the constitutionality of the statue.

V (void or invalid) means that the court has declared the statute invalid.

Some of these abbreviations may be seen in Exhibit 2 which shows page 139 (see lower left-hand corner) from *Shepard's Massacuhsetts Citations.* The part of the volume to be used in "Shepardizing" statutory provisions is always identified by the name of the code at the top of the page in the citator.

Sections of the Massachusetts laws may be identified by the larger numbers in bold-face type preceded by the section symbol. From this example, it may be seen that section 24A of Chapter 74 was amended by Chapter 154 of the 1958 session laws, while a new

[1] Reproduced with permission of the publisher and copyright owner, Shepard's Citations, Inc., Colorado Springs, Colo.

Massachusetts—Massachusetts General Laws Annotated **Ch. 81**

§ 4
A1960C 403
§ 4A
A1960C 403
§ 4B
A1960C 403
§ 5
A1960C 403
§ 6
A1960C 403
§ 7
A1958C 605
A1959C 246
L1959C 477
A1959C 592
A1960C 403
§ 8
A1959C 246
A1960C 403
§ 9
R1958C 605

Ch. 74
335Mas 493
140NE 474
1958C518§3
1960C330§3
§ 1
"Agricultural Education"
335Mas 491
140NE 470
"Industrial Education"
335Mas 491
140NE 470
"Vocational Education"
335Mas 493
140NE 470
§ 24A
A1958C 154
§ 31B
Ad1960C481
§ 42B
A1958C 243
§ 42C
Ad1958C538

Ch. 75
335Mas 493
140NE 474
'56-57AG 45
§ 1
'56-57AG 45
§ 5A
'56-57AG 45
§ 13
A1960C 526
'57-58AG 49
§ 24
'56-57AG 46
§ 26
335Mas 447
140NE 487
§ 27
1958C 456
§ 28
L1958C 456

§ 32
Ad1960C493

Ch. 75A
335Mas 493
140NE 474
§ 2
'56-57AG 82
§ 12
A1958C 538
A1960C 563

Ch. 75B
Ad1960C543
§ 1
Ad1960C543
§ 2
Ad1960C543
§ 3
Ad1960C543
§ 4
Ad1960C543
§ 5
Ad1960C543
§ 6
Ad1960C543
§ 7
Ad1960C543
§ 8
Ad1960C543
§ 9
Ad1960C543
§ 10
Ad1960C543
§ 11
Ad1960C543
§ 12
Ad1960C543
§ 13
Ad1960C543
§ 14
Ad1960C543
§ 15
Ad1960C543
§ 16
Ad1960C543
§ 17
Ad1960C543
§ 18
Ad1960C543
§ 19
Ad1960C543
§ 20
Ad1960C543

Ch. 76
§ 1
'56-57AG 66
§ 5
'56-57AG 67

Ch. 77
44MQ(2)119
§ 13
Rs1960C 313

Ch. 78
Rp1960C429

§ 10
et seq.
38BUR386
§ 16
R1960C 429
§ 17
R1960C 429
§ 18
R1960C 429
§ 19
A1960C 429

TITLE XIII

Ch. 79
L1958C 603
335Mas 80
138NE 609
335Mas 620
142NE 348
335Mas 723
142NE 327
336Mas 56
142NE 391
336Mas 137
143NE 220
336Mas 448
146NE 488
337Mas 308
149NE 227
338Mas 218
154NE 606
338Mas 662
157NE 209
1959AS 734
158NE 349
1959AS1019
159NE 342
1959AS1243
161NE 759
1959AS1287
162NE 266
1960AS 132
164NE 138
1960AS 589
165NE 748
1960AS 759
166NE 904
170NE 355
174FS 454
1958C 212
1958C232§2
1958C242§1
1958C 250
1958C297§4
1958C 353
1958C 371
1958C 384
1958C 418
1958C 420
1958C 472
1958C 473
1958C 474
1958C518§6
1958C 524
1958C 531
1958C532§5
1958C 563
1958C 587
1958C598§5
1958C606§5
1958C 652
1958Res
[C 148
1959C 172
1959C 212
1959C 291
1959C 377
1959C 601
1960C 23
1960C 66
1960C 68
1960C 308
1960C 418
1960C440§4
1960C 450
1960C543§4
1960C635§4
1960C 710
1960 p 575
§ 1
et seq.
1959AS 733
158NE 348
1959AS1287
162NE 265
1960AS 589
165NE 747
§ 1
E1958C 603
335Mas 624
142NE 350
38BUR415
§ 3
E1958C 603
A1959C 626
335Mas 622
142NE 349
44MQ(3) 23
§ 4
E1958C 603
§ 6
335Mas 190
138NE 769
§ 7
174FS 453
§ 8
E1958C 603
A1959C 626
A1960C 49
335Mas 622
142NE 349
174FS 454
44MQ(3) 23
§ 8A
Ad1959C626
44MQ(3) 23
§ 9
E1958C 603
335Mas 623
142NE 347
336Mas 130
143NE 216
44MQ(2) 15
§ 10
E1958C 603
335Mas 624
142NE 347
336Mas 54
142NE 390
336Mas 137
143NE 220
338Mas 218
154NE 605
44MQ(2) 15
§ 12
E1958C 603
A1959C 626
335Mas 81
138NE 609
335Mas 193
138NE 769
335Mas 374
140NE 212
335Mas 598
141NE 384
335Mas 625
142NE 351
335Mas 724
142NE 328
336Mas 54
142NE 390
336Mas 131
143NE 217
338Mas 49
153NE 623
338Mas 218
154NE 605
338Mas 662
157NE 209
1959AS1021
159NE 342
1960AS1092
169NE 904
1960AS1133
170NE 324
162FS 484
44MQ(2) 15
44MQ(3) 24
§ 13
E1958C 603
§ 14
E1958C 603
335Mas 190
138NE 769
335Mas 622
142NE 349
335Mas 723
142NE 327
336Mas 55
142NE 390
336Mas 134
143NE 216
337Mas 433
149NE 905
338Mas 360
155NE 171
1959AS1477
162NE 777
1960AS1133
170NE 324
174FS 453
44MQ(3) 23
§ 16
et seq.
E1958C 603
§ 16
335Mas 622
142NE 349
336Mas 130
143NE 216
174FS 454
§ 22
336Mas 57
142NE 392
174FS 453
44MQ(2) 18
§ 24
et seq.
336Mas 446
146NE 486
§ 32
336Mas 57
142NE 392
1959AS1477
162NE 777
§ 33
1959AS1478
162NE 777
§ 35
335Mas 81
138NE 610
338Mas 48
153NE 623
44MQ(2) 19
§ 37
Rs1960C 298
335Mas 601
141NE 384
1960AS1133
170NE 325
§ 38
44MQ(3) 24
§ 39
A1959C 626
44MQ(3) 23
§ 40
E1958C 606
1958C598§5
§ 41
E1958C 603
§ 42
E1958C 603
§ 43
E1958C 603
§ 44A
E1958C 603
335Mas 598
141NE 381
1960AS 405
165NE 113
§ 44B
336Mas 133
143NE 218
§ 45
174FS 453

Ch. 80
1958C 250
1958C 563
1959C 291
1960C 23
1960C 308
1960C 450
§ 1
L1960C 589
1959C 39
§ 2
L1960C 589
1959C 39
§ 12
337Mas 467
150NE 276
§ 13
A1960C 248
1959C 47

Ch. 80A
1958C242§1
1958C 624
1959C 172

TITLE XIV

Ch. 81
335Mas 625
142NE 351
'56-57AG 91
§ 7
335Mas 625
142NE 351
336Mas 131
143NE 220
338Mas 223
154NE 608
1959AS1021
159NE 342
272F2d 430
44MQ(2) 18
§ 7A
A1960C 183
337Mas 310
149NE 225
§ 7C
335Mas 79
138NE 609
335Mas 625
142NE 351
336Mas 131
143NE 220
1959AS1019
159NE 342
272F2d 430
'56-57AG 91
44MQ(2) 18
§ 7D
'56-57AG 91
§ 7F
Ad1958C582
§ 7G
Ad1960C710
§ 12
335Mas 1
138NE 276
§ 14
1960AS 562
166NE 219
§ 21
335Mas 78
138NE 609
'56-57AG 91

139

Exhibit 2. Photostatic copy of page 139, *Massachusetts Citations, Cases and Statutes*, February, 1961. Reproduced with permission of the publisher and copyright owner, Shepard's Citations, Inc., Colorado Springs, Colo.

section—31B—was added in 1960 by Chapter 481 of the session laws. Also, section 16 of Chapter 78 was repealed by Chapter 429 of the 1960 session laws.

In addition to showing what has happened to each section of the statutes by subsequent legislatures, Shepard's citators show where each section has been cited by a court; *e.g.*, section 21 of Chapter 81 has been cited in 335 Mass. 78, 138 N.E. (2d) 609 and on page 91 of the 1956-57 volume of attorney general's opinions. Unless there is a symbol in front of these references to cases, it means merely that the court referred to that section. If the court, for example, held that a section is constitutional, the reference would be preceded by a "C."

These examples show the practical value of Shepard's Citations to Statutes. (Citators contain citations to the constitution, to state statutes, and to court decisions in the same volume for each state, usually, but they are separately treated in the citators and discussed separately here. In a few states there are separate volumes for statutes and court decisions.)

State department publications of school law which do not use the codification of the state compilation of laws cannot be used with the citators. It was for this reason that recommendation was made that state codes be used for legal research rather than state department publications, unless the state department bulletin follows the same numbering system as is used in the state code.

For laws enacted after the date of the official state code, annual session laws are used and a section of Shepard's Citations to Statutes is devoted to citations to session laws, by years, in the same way that citations to the state code sections are shown in Exhibit 2.

State Law Index. Until 1949, the Library of Congress issued biennially an index to state legislation arranged by subject matter. It was the only publication of its kind where statutory material was compiled by subject matter. Unfortunately no appropriation was made by Congress in 1949 for the continuance of this work and the last issue covers the 1947-1948 biennium. Therefore, statutes must be researched by each state separately. Nowhere is to be found an index to statutes from all states.

Court Decisions

Appellate courts, in some states the intermediate as well as the highest court, record their opinions for future reference and these records are available to the public in the form of so-called "reports." Almost every state publishes its own series of reports. In Exhibit 2 many notations may be found referring to cases reported in the Massachusetts reports, as was mentioned.

If one is interested in a problem at large, he will want to read cases on the subject outside his own state. Thousands of cases are reported each year and without mechanical devices to segregate the cases in point, the task would be impossible. There are several such devices, to be described below.

The American Digest System. The American Digest System is a series of digests of cases from 1658 to date. There are eight units, as follows:

1956 to date: General Digest, Third Series;
1946 to 1956: Sixth Decennial Digest (36 volumes);
1936 to 1946: Fifth Decennial Digest (49 volumes);
1926 to 1936: Fourth Decennial Digest (34 volumes);
1916 to 1926: Third Decennial Digest (29 volumes);
1906 to 1916: Second Decennial Digest (24 volumes);
1896 to 1906: First Decennial Digest (25 volumes);
1658 to 1896: Century Digest.

Cases in each of these units are arranged in the same order according to subject matter. "Schools and School Districts" is in its alphabetical setting. Within each topic the subject matter is logically outlined and each item in the outline is given a number; this number is called the key number. As an illustration of the detail used in classifying the cases for the American Digest System, the outline of topics on "Schools and School Districts" is here reproduced in part.[2] The arabic number in front of each subtopic is its key number.

I. Private Schools and Academies. (1-8).
II. Public Schools. (9-178).
  A. Establishment, School Lands and Funds, and Regulation in General. (9-20).
  B. Creation, Alteration, Existence, and Dissolution of Districts. (21-44).
  C. Government, Officers, and District Meetings. (45-63).
  D. District Property, Contracts, and Liabilities. (64-89.19).
  E. District Debt, Securities, and Taxation. (90-111).
  F. Claims against District, and Actions. (112-126).

[2] Reproduced with permission of the publisher and copyright owner, West Publishing Company, St. Paul, Minn.

G. Teachers. (127-147).

127. Eligibility in general.
128. Teachers' institutes.
129. Certificate or license.
130. ____In general.
131. ____Requisites to appointment or employment.
132. ____Revocation.
133. Employment in general.
133.1. Selection and appointment.
133.2. ____Nomination by district boards.
133.3. ____Recommendation by superintendent of schools.
133.4. ____Civil service laws and examinations.
133.5. Term of employment in general.
133.6. Permanent tenure.
133.7. ____Constitutional and statutory provisions in general.
133.8. ____Purpose of statutes.
133.9. ____Construction and operation of statutes.
133.10. ____Teachers and persons entitled in general.
133.11. ____Length of service and probation.
133.12. ____Substitute and supply teachers.
133.13. ____Schools affected.
133.14. Leave of absence.
133.15. Reappointment.
134. Contracts of employment.
135. ____Making, requisites, and validity.
    (1). Authority to contract in general.
    (2). Authority to bind successors.
    (3). Requisites and validity in general.
    (4). Formal requisites.
    (5). Ratification and estoppel.
136. ____Construction and operation.
137. ____Performance or breach.
138. ____Remedies for enforcement.
139. Resignation and abandonment.
140. Suspension, removal, and reassignment.
141. ____In general.
    (1). In general.
    (2). Authority to remove or discharge in general.
    (3). Contracts reserving right.
    (4). Grounds for removal or suspension.
    (5). Proceedings and review.
    (6). Reinstatement.
142. ____Actions for damages.
143. Compensation.
144. ____In general.
    (1). Right to compensation in general.
    (2). Effect of closing of school because of contagious disease.
    (3). Effect of removal, suspension, or abandonment of employment.

(4). Rate or amount of compensation.
(5). Payment, and orders therefor.
145. ____Actions.
146. Pensions.
147. Duties and liabilities.

H. Pupils, and Conduct and Discipline of Schools.
148. Nature of right to instruction in general.
148½. Aid to indigent children.
149. Eligibility.
150. ____In general.
151. ____Race or color.
152. ____Age.
153. ____Residence.
154. ____Assignment or admission to particular schools.
155. Proceedings to compel admission.
156. Health regulations.
157. In general.
158. ____Vaccination.
(1). In general.
(2). Existence of epidemic.
159. Payment for tuition.
159½. Transportation of pupils to and from schools or provisions in lieu thereof.
160. Compulsory attendance.
161. Truants and truant officers and schools.
162. School terms, vacations, and holidays.
163. Grades or classes and departments.
164. Curriculum and courses of study.
165. Religious instruction and reading of Scriptures.
166. Textbooks.
167. ____Selection or adoption and change.
168. ____Duty to furnish.
169. Control of pupils and discipline in general.
170. Rules and regulations.
171. ____Authority to make.
172. ____Reasonableness and validity.
172½. ____Construction and operation.
173. Violation of rules and offenses.
174. Punishment.
175. ____In general.
176. ____Corporal punishment.
177. ____Expulsion or suspension.
178. Graduation, and diploma or certificate.

Thus, the American Digest System constitutes a device for finding all of the cases on a point among the thousands of cases reported each year. The System consists of short digests of each case arranged in the order of the outline of topics. Exhibit 3 shows a page from Volume

26 in which "Schools and School Districts" is to be found in the sixth Decennial Digest, covering the period 1946-1956. The number of the subtopic in the outline is identified by a tiny key in front of it, and for this reason it is referred to as the "key number." At the beginning of each digest is the name of the state in bold-face type. At the end of each digest is the citation to the case, its name, and where it may be found.

Exhibit 3 shows the digests of *all* cases decided between 1946 and 1956 in which the topic "Selection and appointment" of teachers—key number 133.1—was an issue. The first case listed under this key number arose in New York and was decided in the Supreme Court of the United States. It was *Adler* v. *Board of Education of City of New York* which may be read at 72 S. Ct. 380, or at 342 U.S. 485, or at 96 L. Ed. 517. This digest is followed by the digest of a case from Alabama and cases from other states are listed alphabetically by state.

The American Digest System includes a Table of Cases which gives for each case the exact title, alphabetically listed, and all the places where it may be found to be read, also the topic and the key numbers of every point of law decided in each case and whether it has been affirmed, reversed, or modified. From the Table of Cases, then, the key numbers of a familiar case may be noted, and other cases can be found in the digests by looking for those identified by the same key numbers.

There is also a subject matter index to the American Digest System. It is called the "Descriptive Word Index." This index uses nonlegal terms as well as legal terminology and contains innumerable cross references. Key numbers identify the references, and it is possible to discover by this index under what key number a point has been digested.

Any particular case contains more than one point which is indexed with a key number. For example, an action by a dismissed teacher for reinstatement might be indexed under Removal, Compensation, Contract, and Mandamus. Each of these points has a different key number. Therefore, in the Descriptive Word Index and in the digests themselves, the case may be indexed in more than one place depending upon the various points involved in the case. In the reports of actual opinions, however, the case appears only once in each report although headnotes at the beginning before the opinion itemize the points of law involved under all the key numbers.

Act of 1939, P.L. 482, as amended by the Act of 1947, P.L. 646.—Weiland v. Stull, 16 Cambria 249.

Pa.Com.Pl. The number of teachers to be hired is a matter for the internal management of the board of school directors under the supervision of the Department of Public Instruction; and unless the School Code contains a plain mandate requiring the employment of a specified number of teachers on a basis of calculated units, the court may not interfere with the discretion of the board exercised in accordance with advice from the Department of Public Instruction.—Caperelli v. Winton Borough, School Dist., 53 Lack.Jur. 269.

The fact that the state by mathematical computation based on the number of pupil-days provides state aid on the basis of calculated reimbursement units does not warrant the court in holding that the school district must employ the number of teachers necessary to fill a mathematical quota authorized because the school district is entitled to such reimbursement units.—Caperelli v. Winton Borough, School Dist., 53 Lack.Jur. 269.

Pa.Com.Pl. Although the term "professional employee" includes teachers actively assigned to continuous classroom work, it is not exclusive as to such assignments.—McAndrew v. Throop Borough, School Dist. of, 56 Lack.Jur. 201.

Wash. Teachers are employees of district which employs them, and are not public or state officers.—State ex rel. Mary M. Knight School Dist. No. 311, Mason County v. Wanamaker, 281 P.2d 846.

W.Va. Statute prescribing method of employment of teachers in schools of a county school district is exclusive, and nomination by County Superintendent is an indispensable prerequisite to execution of a valid teaching contract between the County Board of Education and a teacher. Code, 18-4-10(2, 3) as amended 18-5-4 as amended 18-7-1 as amended.—Cochran v. Trussler, 89 S.E. 2d 306.

⇨133.1. Selection and appointment

U.S.N.Y. School authorities have right and duty to screen officials, teachers, and employees as to their fitness to maintain integrity of schools as part of ordered society.—Adler v. Board of Ed. of City of New York, 72 S.Ct. 380, 342 U.S. 485, 96 L.Ed. 517.

In employment of officials and teachers for school system, state may properly inquire into company they keep and, when determining fitness and loyalty of such persons, may consider organisations and persons with whom they associate.—Adler v. Board of Ed. of City of New York, 72 S.Ct. 380, 342 U.S. 485, 96 L.Ed. 517.

Ala. The "administrative functions" exercised by a board of education in public school system include the hiring of teachers, their assignment in the school system, and the management and control of school property.—State ex rel. Steele v. Board of Ed. of Fairfield, 40 So.2d 689.

Fla. Power to select and nominate teachers for public schools is vested in the trustees.—State ex rel. Lawson v. Cherry, 47 So.2d 768.

Ill.App. No person has the right to demand to be employed as a teacher, and School Board has absolute right to decline to employ an applicant for any reason.—Halfacre v. Board of Ed. of School Dist. No. 167, 73 N.E.2d 124, 331 Ill.App. 404.

District School Board of Education was entitled to reject application for a teacher's position without giving any reason therefor, notwithstanding that applicant was the only applicant for the position holding a valid teacher's certificate.—Halfacre v. Board of Ed. of School Dist. No. 167, 73 N.E.2d 124, 331 Ill.App. 404.

Ky. An illegal appointment as high school principal could not serve as foundation of appointee's claim to continued employment. KRS 160.380.—Beverly v. Highfield, 209 S.W.2d 739, 307 Ky. 179.

Mass. The powers of school committee include the employment of janitors and custodians as well as teachers and the absolute right to fix their salaries, and no other officer has authority over the maintenance of schoolhouses. G.L. (Ter.Ed.) c. 71, §§ 37, 68 as amended.—Molinari v. City of Boston, 130 N.E.2d 925.

Mont. Under statute, no person can be employed to teach in public schools without a contract with board of school trustees, and so-called teachers' tenure act does not eliminate necessity of having a contract; the only effect of tenure act being to renew teacher's existing contract for another year by operation of law after election for third consecutive year unless notice specified in statute is given. Rev.Codes 1935, § 1015, subd. 2; § 1075.—Eastman v. School Dist. No. 1 of Lewis and Clark County, 180 P.2d 472, 120 Mont. 63.

N.Y.App.Div. A petition filed in 1946 for declaration that petitioner was a regular member of faculty of city college of New York with full tenure was not filed late insofar as it sought to compel performance of duty which the Board of Higher Education had not refused to perform, but was filed late insofar as petitioner sought to review propriety of determination in 1942 that eligible lists of former high school teachers would not be applicable for positions in municipal colleges. Education Law, § 1143-c, subd. 9; Civil Practice Act, § 1286.—Trilling v. Board of Higher Ed. of City of New York, 67 N.Y.S.2d 572, 190 Misc. 52.

N.C. Election of a principal or teacher by school committee of district in a county administrative unit has no validity until such election has been approved by both the county superintendent of schools and county board of education. G.S. §§ 115-112, 115-354.—Iredell County Bd. of Ed. v. Dickson, 70 S.E.2d 14, 235 N.C. 359.

Resolution adopted by county board of education in meeting assembled after close of school term supporting any action taken by district school committee in electing a principal for specified school undertook to give district school committee carte blanche in the premises, and not to confer retroactive approval on previously attempted dismissal or rejection of principal. G.S. §§ 115-354, 115-359.—Iredell County Bd. of Ed. v. Dickson, 70 S.E.2d 14, 235 N.C. 359.

Re-election of principal by school committee of district in a county administrative unit without approval of county superintendent of schools or county board of education was without any validity in law and hence under statute, principal's contract of employment automatically continued in force for ensuing year, though he failed to give notice to county superintendent of schools of acceptance of renewed employment within 10 days after notice of re-election. G.S. §§ 115-37, 115-354.—Iredell County Bd. of Ed. v. Dickson, 70 S.E.2d 14, 235 N.C. 359.

N.Y.Sup. The determination of Board of Higher Education of City of New York, upon abolishing high school which had been operated to prepare students for entrance into college of City of New York, that preferred lists established upon abolition of the high school should not be deemed applicable to positions in municipal colleges was discretionary with the board. Education Law, § 1143-c, subd. 9.—Trilling v. Board of Higher Ed. of City of New York, 67 N.Y.S.2d 572, 190 Misc. 52.

Where Board of Higher Education of City of New York upon abolishing high school which had been operated to prepare students for entrance to City College established preferred eligible list pursuant to statute which required such lists to be established for three years, and during such period no one was appointed to any educational unit in disregard of the list, a former teacher in high school was not entitled as matter of right to appointment to faculty of city college. Education Law, § 1143-c, subd. 9.—Trilling v. Board of Higher Ed. of City of New York, 67 N.Y.S.2d 572, 190 Misc. 52.

Ohio Com.Pl. Statutory provision that if a clerk of a board of education is absent from any meeting of board, members present shall choose one of their number to serve in his place pro tempore, provision that clerk shall record proceedings of each meeting and provision that on a motion to adopt a resolution to employ a superintendent or teacher, clerk of board shall publicly call roll of members composing board and enter on records names of those voting aye and names of those voting no, and mandatory and noncompliance therewith by a board invalidates its proceedings. Gen.Code, §§ 4834-1 to 4834-3.—Schafer v. Board of Ed. of Alliance City School Dist., Stark County, 94 N.E.2d 112.

The words "to employ" a superintendent or teacher in statute providing that, on a motion to adopt a resolution to employ a superintendent or teacher, clerk of board shall publicly call roll of members composing board and enter on records names of those voting aye and names of those voting no, embody and encompass words "not to employ," "to accept or not to accept a resignation" and "to retain or not to retain" a superintendent of schools. Gen.Code, § 4834-1.—Schafer v. Board of Ed. of Alliance City School Dist., Stark County, 94 N.E.2d 112.

Pa.Com.Pl. The employment of a teacher as a "professional employee" of a school district must be made, and salary fixed, by the affirmative vote of the majority of all the members of the board of directors, duly recorded on the minutes, showing how each member voted.—Felix v. Fairfield Tp. School Dist., Bd. of Directors, 32 West. 207.

Wash. Under statute providing for employment of school teachers by school boards, the Legislature has left question of employment solely within discretion of school board and applicant, and no district can be forced to enter into a contract of employment with teacher against will of majority of board of directors, nor can applicant be forced to teach school in any district against her will. RCW 28.58.100 (1).—State ex rel. Mary M. Knight School Dist. No. 311, Mason County v. Wanamaker, 281 P.2d 846.

⇨133.2. —— Nomination by district boards

Fla. Board of trustees of school district had no discretion under statute to reject recommendation of county superintendent and refuse to nominate district supervising principal to board of public instruction for reappointment, except for good cause shown. F.S.A. §§ 230.01 et seq., 230.33(7) (c), 230.43(1), 231.35.—Armistead v. State ex rel. Smyth, 41 So.2d 879.

The board of trustees for each school district is vested by Constitution with the power to nominate teachers for the district. F.S.A.Const. art. 12, § 10.—Armistead v. State ex rel. Smyth, 41 So.2d 879.

Exhibit 3. Photostatic copy of page 1578 in Volume 26 of the *Sixth Decennial Digest*. Reproduced with permission of the publisher and copyright owner, West Publishing Company, St. Paul, Minn.

From the American Digest System one compiles a bibliography of cases for further study. The digests in the American Digest System aid in determining whether a particular case is likely to be in point; they may be used in classifying cases to fit into a topical outline to be followed in the research study. But, this is just the first step in making a legal study. The digests are only these short paragraphs on each point in the case, as shown in Exhibit 3. In order to know their application, it is necessary to read the entire opinion of the court in the reports. The holding of a case cannot be cited on the basis of the digests alone. Doing so is an error of many inexperienced school-law researchers. The opinion must be read in its entirety.

Court opinions may be found in the state reports, in the National Reporter System, or possibly in the Annotated Reports which are to be described later.

National Reporter System. The National Reporter System includes all cases from all courts of record in all states and gives the actual opinion of the court in each. Using the National Reporter System, it is possible to read all the cases in all the states on a particular point. The System is divided into nine geographical sections, for publication and citation purposes:

The Atlantic Reporter, abbreviated "Atl." or "A. (2d)," covers Maine, New Hampshire, Vermont, Connecticut, New Jersey, Pennsylvania, Delaware, and Maryland.

The Northeastern Reporter, abbreviated "N.E." or "N.E. (2d)," covers Massachusetts, Rhode Island, New York, Ohio, Indiana, and Illinois.

The Southeastern Reporter, abbreviated "S.E." or "S.E. (2d)," covers Virginia, West Virginia, North Carolina, South Carolina, and Georgia.

The Southern Reporter, abbreviated "So." or "So. (2d)," covers Florida, Alabama, Mississippi, and Louisiana.

The Southwestern Reporter, abbreviated "S.W." or "S.W. (2d)," covers Kentucky, Tennessee, Missouri, Arkansas, and Texas.

The Pacific Reporter, abbreviated "Pac." or "P. (2d)," covers Montana, Wyoming, Idaho, Kansas, Colorado, Oklahoma, New Mexico, Utah, Arizona, Nevada, Washington, Oregon, and California.

The Northwestern Reporter, abbreviated "N.W." or "N.W. (2d)," covers Michigan, Wisconsin, Iowa, Minnesota, North Dakota, South Dakota, and Nebraska.

The National Reporter System also includes the Supreme Court Reporter covering cases decided in the Supreme Court of the United States; the Federal Reporter covering cases decided in the Federal Circuit Court of Appeals; the Federal Supplement covering cases decided in the lower federal courts; and Federal Rules Decisions covering in full opinions of the United States District Courts that are not designated for publication in the Federal Supplement, involving the Federal Rules of Civil Procedure since 1939 and involving the Federal Rules of Criminal Procedures since 1946.

New York State is reported not only in the Northeastern Reporter but in the New York Supplement which was started in 1887 covering certain New York courts only. The California Reporter was first published in 1960. California cases prior to 1960 are found in the Pacific Reporter.

Several volumes in each reporter series are issued each year. Prior to the publication of each volume, the cases are published in weekly bulletins with paper bindings, called "Advance Sheets." These weekly bulletins enable one to read a case without waiting for the publication of the reporter in its bound form. With the use of the Advance Sheets a problem may usually be followed to within a month of any current date. It takes at least a month for a decision to be released by the court, processed, and reported in the weekly bulletins.

The case material in this textbook is excerpted from the court decisions which are reported in the state reports and in the National Reporter System. The latter need not be illustrated at this point since it is identical to that material. It may be mentioned, however, that at the beginning of each decision editors of the National Reporter System have inserted digests of points in the case, reproduced from the American Digest System (see Exhibit 3). These digests at the beginning of each case in the National Reporter System are not part of the court's opinion unless they are shown separately under the heading of "Syllabus of the Court." Usually the name of the judge who wrote the opinion appears at the beginning of the opinion; any language preceding this point is not part of the opinion.

Annotated Reports. Since there are many cases on some problems, one may wish to read only the leading cases, and omit those which involve identical problems and are decided on the basis of the decisions in leading cases. The Annotated Reports make this possible. It is a series of selected cases from all states. Cases dealing with purely local law are eliminated as are also decisions on problems already well settled. The cases included are those which are new or deal with questions on which there is conflict of legal opinion. Some other cases are included because they represent outstanding legal reasoning or review the authorities on a question.

The Annotated Reports consist of seven series including early English and American decisions. Except for historical studies, only the latest series need be used in school-law research; that is, the *American Law Reports* (abbreviated "A.L.R.") which began in 1919. About six volumes appear each year. Alphabetical indexes are furnished as well as indexes to cases and to annotations.

The word "annotations" is here used in a different sense than formerly in this text. The name of this series of law books, Annotated Reports, is taken from notes which follow most of the cases reported. These notes are called annotations. This series is used primarily because of the annotations, although it can be used for reading of the opinion also. The annotations review the substance of what has been decided in other cases on the same point.

Indexes to A.L.R. Annotations are so well done that the numerical system is of secondary importance. However, it does facilitate research if one can scan for a particular topic by number. The outline of topics used by the editors of A.L.R. follows:[3]

I. IN GENERAL
II. SCHOOL DISTRICTS, IN GENERAL
III. PROPERTY AND BUILDINGS
IV. LIABILITY OF SCHOOL DISTRICT OR AUTHORITIES
V. CONTRACTS; FUNDS AND EXPENDITURES; INDEBTEDNESS
VI. SCHOOL TAXES
VII. ADMINISTRATIVE OFFICERS AND BOARDS
VIII. PUBLIC MEETINGS; ELECTIONS
IX. TEACHERS AND PRINCIPALS
  Sec. 30 Generally.
  Sec. 31 Selection, appointment, and term of employment.
  Sec. 32 Contracts of employment.
  Sec. 33 ____Power of school authorities to bind successors by.
  Sec. 33.5 Tenure and tenure statutes, generally.
  Sec. 34 Qualification, generally.

[3] Reproduced with permission of the publishers and copyright owners, The Lawyers Co-operative Publishing Company, Rochester, N. Y., and Bancroft-Whitney Company, San Francisco, Calif.

Sec. 35 License or certificate.
Sec. 36 ____As requisite to appointment or employment.
Sec. 37 ____Revocation or suspension.
Sec. 38 Compensation.
Sec. 39 ____While school is closed.
Sec. 41 Transfer.
Sec. 42 Suspension; dismissal; resignation; reinstatement.
Sec. 43 ____Grounds and procedure for.
Sec. 44 ____Actions for damages for wrongful suspension or dismissal.
Sec. 45 Liability of.
Sec. 48 Pensions and retirement funds. [See Pensions and Retirement Funds, sec. 7.]

X. PUPILS
Sec. 49 Generally.
Sec. 50 Admission generally; residence.
Sec. 51 Scholarships.
Sec. 52 Separation or discrimination by reason of race, color, or religion.
Sec. 55 Health regulations.
Sec. 57 ____Vaccination or inoculation.
Sec. 58 Transportation of.
Sec. 59 Compulsory attendance.
Sec. 60 Control over; patriotic ritual; discipline.
Sec. 61 Secret societies; fraternities and sororities.
Sec. 62 Suspension or expulsion; reinstatement.
Sec. 63 Graduation; right to diploma.

XI. TEXTBOOKS; SUPPLIES AND EQUIPMENT
Sec. 64 Textbooks.
Sec. 65 Supplies and equipment.

XII. INSTRUCTION; CURRICULUM
Sec. 66 Generally.
Sec. 67 Sectarianism; religious teaching.
Sec. 68 Thrift system and instruction.
Sec. 69 Physical education; athletics.

XIII. PRIVATE AND PAROCHIAL SCHOOLS

Some annotations are lengthy, and all except the shortest ones are preceded by an outline of the annotation. An example of an outline of an annotation on a school-law case is given below. It follows the report of the case *Mitchell v. Consolidated School District*, __ Wash. (2d) __, 135 P. (2d) 79. The annotation is cited 146 A.L.R. 625. The outline at the beginning of the annotation is shown here:[4]

[4] Reproduced with permission of the publishers and copyright owners, The Lawyers Co-operative Publishing Company, Rochester, N. Y., and Bancroft-Whitney Company, San Francisco, Calif.

Annotation (p. 625-638)
Transportation of school pupils at expense of public
[Schools #58]

I. Power to provide transportation in the absence of express statute, 625.
II. Constitutionality of statutes expressly providing for transportation:
  a. Generally, 625.
     [No later decisions herein.]
  b. Objection of diversion of school funds, 626.
  c. Classification, discrimination, uniformity, 627.
  d. Other objections, 628.
III. Powers, duties, and rights under statutes:
  a. Extent of power conferred:
    1. Generally, 629.
    2. Place or character of school, 629.
    3. Outside school activities, 631.
       [No later decisions herein.]
  b. Discretionary or mandatory, 631.
  c. Abuse of discretion, 633.
  d. Who entitled to transporation, 633.
  e. Measuring distance, 633.
     [No later decisions herein.]
  f. Sufficiency of transporation:
    1. Part-way transportation, 633.
    2. Character of conveyance, 634.
    3. Shelters, 634.
       [No later decisions herein.]
  g. Contracts for transportation, 634.
  h. Matters relating to remedy, 638.
     [No later decisions herein.]
  i. Miscellaneous, 638.

This annotation supplements those in 63 A.L.R. 413 and 118 A.L.R. 806.

This annotation covers the problem of pupil transportation exhaustively so far as case law is concerned; any topics not directly related to the items of the outline are cross-referenced to other annotations. The annotation in 146 A.L.R., outline of which is quoted above, reviews all the judicial authorities since the former annotations on the subject and shows the existing current state of the law. Notice that in this annotation no decisions are included under several subtopics which had been reviewed in the former annotations. This means that since the former annotations there have been no decisions involving these points.

Annotations such as this example are extremely useful in obtaining a general understanding of a point, or in gathering together loose ends of a topic after having read many, and possibly conflicting, cases.

Whenever a new decision warrants it, an annotation is published to bring the entire topic up to date. In the example, the previous annotation was 118 A.L.R. 806, and, before that, 63 A.L.R. 413. Thus by tracing back the several annotations on a topic it is possible to study the history of a problem over the years. The same outline is used in each annotation on a particular topic, but information found in one annotation is not repeated in a subsequent one.

Shepard's Citations to Cases. When a bibliography of cases has been made from the American Digest System, and the judicial opinions have been read in the state reports or in the National Reporter System, and the annotations on the topic, if any, studied in the Annotated Reports, the next question is whether there have been later cases which followed, disapproved, modified, or reversed these decisions. Shepard's Citations to Cases is the tool used for this purpose.

Each time any case is cited in another decision, Shepard's Citations make note of that fact with appropriate abbreviations to indicate what happened. A few examples of these abbreviations are listed here:[5]

a (affirmed) means that the same case was affirmed on appeal.

D (dismissed) means that appeal of the same case was dismissed.

m (modified) means that the same case was modified on appeal.

r (reversed) means that the same case was reversed on appeal.

j (dissenting opinion) means that the citation is found in the opinion of dissenting judges.

o (overruled) means that the court expressly rejected the ruling in the cited case as being no longer controlling.

With these abbreviations in mind, study of Exhibit 4 will show the usefulness of Shepard's Citations. One section of the state citator is devoted to court decisions. The geographical areas of the National Reporter System are also separately published in the form of citations to cases such as in Exhibit 4.

The page exhibited includes cases in volumes 155 and 156 of the Northeastern Reporter, Second Series. The numbers, such as **—682—**, refer to the page in the respective volume. Occasionally, an opinion

[5] Reproduced with permission of the publisher and copyright owner, Shepard's Citations, Inc., Colorado Springs, Colo.

NORTHEASTERN REPORTER, 2d SERIES Vol. 156

—682—
Case 1
(168OS 470)
s155NE 494
—682—
Case 2
a160NE 311
—686—
(106OA 488)
D153NE 674
s144NE 501
—690—
(107OA 473)
—698—
(108OA229)
—702—
(108OA 457)
—708—
D158NE 379
155NE 1497
—709—
(108OA 514)
—713—
18A2 352s
—736—
14A21242s
—745—
158NE 2164
14A2 224s
—754—
(338Mas473)
158NE 1142
164NE 1311
167NE 1758
—758—
(338Mas435)
160NE 3113
—762—
(338Mas442)
s143NE 196
—767—
(338Mas791)
29A2 911s
—768—
(338Mas793)
22A21176s
—770—
(338Mas421)
166NE 5700
—775—
(338Mas368)
158NE 5495
158NE10495
d162NE 1831
Wis
99NW 160
—781—
(338Mas792)
—782—
(338Mas793)
24A2 194s
—783—
(338Mas481)
163NE 9266
—787—
(338Mas468)
—791—
(338Mas450)
157NE11222
164NE 5316
167NE 156
—798—
Case 1
(338Mas793)
46A2 9s

—798—
Case 2
(338Mas460)
—800—
(338Mas790)
—801—
(338Mas792)
—803—
(338Mas465)
46A2 404s
—805—
(338Mas791)
25A2 364s
—806—
(338Mas463)
162NE 119
162NE 219
162NE 2813
—808—
(338Mas790)
—809—
(201IlA224)
163NE 1232
—814—
(201IlA306)
—815—
(201IlA235)
—819—
(201IlA309)
—820—
(201IlA309)
—821*—
(201IlA244)
r162NE 428
37A2 7s
—825—
(201IlA310)
—826—
(201IlA306)
—827—
(201IlA288)
165NE 2740
71A2 91n
71A2 418n
71A2 161n
—829—
(201IlA311)
—830—
(201IlA201)
—832—
(201IlA303)
—833—
(201IlA192)
—838—
(201IlA307)
a163NE 523
—839*—
(201IlA305)
—841—
(201IlA555)
r163NE 89
s362US 968
s 4LE 900
s 80SC 955
68A21448n
—844—
(201IlA370)
—847—
(201IlA308)
—848*—
(201IlA332)
166NE 1621
49A2 797s
—850*—
(201IlA304)

—853—
(5NY134)
(182S2d 1)
s160S2d 152
s171S2d 717
166NE 5321
199S2d 536
185S2d 949
185S2d 990
190S2d 601
196S2d 789
199S2d 155
201S2d1005
203S2d 498
203S2d 993
—859—
Case 1
(5NY858)
(182S2d 9)
s174S2d 230
s176S2d 957
—859—
Case 2
(5NY859)
(182S2d 9)
s163NE 670
s194S2d 922
s177S2d 880
s178S2d 621
—860—
(5NY859)
(182S2d 10)
s140NE 875
s159S2d 983
s158NE 855
s186S2d 284
s150S2d 34
s152S2d 427
s168S2d 307
s169S2d 897
s174S2d 970
s176S2d 938
s176S2d 946
s178S2d 636
—861—
Case 1
(5NY859)
(182S2d 12)
s161NE 217
s190S2d1005
s175S2d 422
s177S2d1010
s178S2d 620
—861—
Case 2
(5NY860)
(182S2d 13)
s174S2d 947
—862—
Case 1
(5NY860)
(182S2d 13)
s156NE 921
s183S2d 566
s175S2d 579
s359US 997
s 3LE 985
s 79SC 1132
—862—
Case 2
(5NY861)
(182S2d 14)
s151NE 90
s174S2d 658
s152NE 657

s177S2d 696
s158NE 122
s185S2d 259
s159NE 697
s188S2d 211
s161NE 740
s191S2d 956
s170S2d 979
—863—
Case 1
(5NY861)
(182S2d 14)
s159NE 211
s186S2d 668
s168S2d 937
s174S2d 487
—863—
Case 2
(5NY862)
(182S2d 15)
s170S2d 852
—864—
(5NY863)
(182S2d 16)
s173S2d 927
—865—
Case 1
(5NY865)
(182S2d 17)
s157S2d 391
s162S2d 80
s171S2d 674
—865—
Case 2
(5NY867)
(182S2d 18)
s153NE 729
s179S2d 97
s170S2d 423
—866—
Case 1
(5NY869)
(182S2d 18)
s148NE 315
s171S2d 104
s154NE 564
s180S2d 308
s167S2d 425
s168S2d 607
—866—
Case 2
(5NY870)
(182S2d 19)
s177S2d1018
—867—
Case 1
(5NY870)
(182S2d 20)
s157NE 717
s184S2d 841
s176S2d 240
—867—
Case 2
(5NY870)
(182S2d 20)
s159NE 206
s186S2d 661
s175S2d 570
—867—
Case 3
(5NY870)
(182S2d 21)
s158NE 512
s185S2d 822

—868—
Case 1
(5NY871)
(182S2d 21)
s154NE 138
s179S2d 859
s158NE 124
s185S2d 262
s159NE 704
s188S2d 222
—868—
Case 2
(5NY871)
(182S2d 21)
—868—
Case 3
(5NY871)
(182S2d 22)
s159NE 677
s188S2d 184
s160NE 128
s188S2d1001
s168NE 705
s203S2d 900
s361US 874
s 4LE 113
s 80SC 137
—868—
Case 4
(5NY871)
(182S2d 22)
s174S2d 447
—869—
Case 1
(5NY871)
(182S2d 22)
s153NE 734
s179S2d 105
s166S2d 492
s175S2d1016
s359US 1004
s 3LE 1032
s 79SC 1143
—869—
Case 2
(5NY872)
(182S2d 23)
s154NE 570
s180S2d 316
s175S2d 557
—870—
Case 1
(5NY874)
(182S2d 24)
s154NE 574
s180S2d 322
s170S2d1010
s175S2d1010
s359US 994
s 3LE 982
s 79SC 1127
165NE 174
197S2d 155
—870—
Case 2
(5NY875)
(182S2d 25)
s173S2d 665
s175S2d 154
191S2d 886
203S2d 280
—871—
(5NY876)
(182S2d 26)

s153NE 733
s179S2d 103
164NE 721
196S2d 703
166NE 862
200S2d 72
168NE 519
203S2d 73
—873—
(338Mas518)
162NE 263
26A2 610s
—874—
(338Mas794)
—876—
(338Mas514)
29A2 731s
—879—
(338Mas401)
—882—
(338Mas795)
—884—
(168OS 391)
50A21029s
69A21383n
—889—
(168OS 482)
159NE 1229
169NE 1456
—897—
(168OS 445)
158NE 1570
163NE 2782
—898—
(168OS 410)
s153NE 711
—904—
(168OS 471)
s153NE 190
q164NE 7165
f166NE 4229
—909—
(168OS 418)
f167NE 1784
—917—
(168OS 398)
53A2 850s
—922—
(168OS 481)
—923—
(168OS 468)
s360US 907
s 3LE 1258
s 79SC 1286
s361US 856
s 4LE 98
s 80SC 47
—925—
(106OA 517)
s151NE 797
s154NE 83
s155NE 468
21A2 643s

Vol. 156

—1*—
(201IlA292)
—4*—
(201IlA279)

s142NE 747
f163NE 8576
—6*—
(201IlA266)
cc125NE 476
—9—
(201IlA259)
—12—
(201IlA311)
—13—
(201IlA282)
s150NE 581
—16—
(201IlA271)
—21—
(338Mas502)
158NE 1482
—24—
(338Mas531)
158NE 3467
162NE 2798
165NE 3912
—30—
(338Mas507)
—34—
(338Mas488)
13A21409s
—38—
(338Mas796)
—39—
(338Mas795)
—41—
(338Mas542)
165NE 5107
42A21319s
—44—
(338Mas494)
60A21146s
—49—
(338Mas526)
168NE 1276
21A2 611s
Ore
341P2d 118
—52—
(338Mas547)
157NE 8883
158NE 141
166NE 5921
168NE 869
—57—
(338Mas520)
18A21010s
—61—
(338Mas554)
162NE 2787
27A21348s
—69—
(5NY142)
(182S2d361)
s162S2d 833
s171S2d 715
204S2d 569
—71—
(5NY147)
(182S2d365)
s175S2d 862
188S2d 800
203S2d 223
—87—
163NE 4579
168NE10210
168NE11210

—111—
(168OS 458)
158NE 1725
—113—
(168OS 447)
(70A21241)
s146NE 454
s167NE 515
—121—
(168OS 431)
s145NE 844
164NE 6572
Calif
8CaR282
Fla
114So2d 434
—131—
(168OS 461)
p164NE 417
167NE 3363
—136—
(168OS 478)
—138—
D162NE 177
D168NE 876
—153—
(107OA 166)
—155—
(106OA 544)
—156—
s154NE 87
—159—
15A2 170s
—162—
34A2 372s
—164—
(106OA 541)
—170—
169NE 662
—175—
155NE 1525
—176—
D147NE 856
a156NE 190
s358US 283
s 3LE 312
s 79SC 297
—190—
D147NE 856
s156NE 176
s163NE 383
s358US 283
s 3LE 312
s 79SC 297
—198—
a164NE 759
—202—
D154NE 822
s359US 988
s 3LE 934
s 79SC 940
—217—
(201IlA343)
—222—
(201IlA297)
16A2 3s
—225—
(201IlA336)
163NE 1108
—229—
Case 1
(201IlA477)
Continued

* Illinois Appellate Court Cases when Certiorari or Leave to Appeal Denied

483

Exhibit 4. Photostatic copy of page 483 of the *Northeastern Reporter Citator,* January 1961. Reproduced with permission of the publisher and copyright owner, Shepard's Citations, Inc., Colorado Springs, Colo.

is so short that two cases appear on the same page of the reporter; this situation is illustrated by the first two cases in Exhibit 4. The small "s" before 155 N. E. (2d) 494 under Case 1 indicates that another opinion in the first case on page 682 of volume 155 of the Northeastern Reporter, Second Series, may be found on page 494 of that volume. The parentheses around 168 OS 470 means that this case appears on page 470 of volume 168 of the state reports as well as on page 682 of the Northeastern Reporter. Case 2 on page 682 of volume 155 was affirmed in a case which may be found on page 311 of volume 160 of the Northeastern Reporter, Second Series. The case appearing on page 6 of volume 156 of the Northeastern Reporter, Second Series, is connected with another case which may be found on page 476 of volume 125 of the Northeastern Reporter, Second Series, as indicated by the symbol "cc." The case, 156 N.E. (2d) 190 was dismissed at 147 N.E. (2d) 856, was affirmed at 156 N.E. (2d) 190, and went to the Supreme Court as shown by the three references to reports of opinions of that Court.

Corpus Juris Secundum. Corpus Juris Secundum, abbreviated "C.J.S.," is the second series of a many-volumed publication of case law principles reported in encyclopedic form. Textual matter provides a running account, and copious footnotes give citations to cases in point. The material is classified according to subject matter and the topic "Schools and School Districts" appears in volumes 78 and 79. Pocket parts keep *Corpus Juris Secundum* up to date.

Each subject in *Corpus Juris Secundum* is outlined in detail at the beginning of its treatment, and each subtopic in the outline is given a number which is used in the discussion to identify the subtopic. There are 512 subtopics in "Schools and School Districts," a few of which are given herewith:[6]

I. DEFINITIONS AND CLASSIFICATION OF SCHOOLS, secs. 1-2.
II. PRIVATE SCHOOLS, secs. 3-11.
III. PUBLIC SCHOOLS, secs. 12-512.
  A. In General, secs. 12-15.
  B. School Lands and School Funds, secs. 16-22.
  C. School Districts and other Local School Organizations, secs. 23-82.
  D. Administration, Government, and Officers, secs. 83-143.
  E. Agents and Employees, secs. 144-153.

---

[6] Reproduced with permission of the publisher and copyright owner, The American Law Book Company, Brooklyn, N. Y.

the certificate for use in that county[50] and to make it exempt from collateral attack.[51]

§ 168. —— Conclusiveness as Evidence; Collateral Attack

A teacher's certificate is prima facie evidence of the teacher's qualifications, and of the fact that the members of the board or committee issuing such certificate have properly performed their duty as to the manner and requisites of their issuing it. In the absence of fraud it cannot be collaterally impeached.

A teacher's certificate is prima facie evidence of the teacher's qualifications[52] and of the fact that the members of the board or committee issuing such certificate have properly performed their duty as to the manner and requisites of their issuing it.[53] In the absence of fraud it cannot be collaterally impeached,[54] as, for example, in a suit by a teacher to recover wages after being dismissed,[55] or after destruction of the school by fire and failure of the board to provide other quarters,[56] or in a suit between contestants to try title to the office of state superintendent of public instruction[57] or county superintendent of schools.[58]

§ 169. Attendance at Teachers' Institute

Attendance at a teachers' institute may be necessary before the teacher can be lawfully permitted to teach.

Where the statute so provides, attendance at a teachers' institute for the period designated is necessary before the teacher can be lawfully permitted to teach[59] unless the teacher has been excused therefrom by a proper school official,[60] which excuse may be given orally in the absence of statutory requirement to the contrary.[61] A statute which provides for the collection of annual fees from applicants for teachers' certificates for the support of teachers' institutes is valid.[62]

2. Selection, Appointment, or Election

§ 170. In General

Appointment is generally a prerequisite to employment as a teacher, principal, or superintendent; and the matter of appointment of such school employees is, subject to constitutional restrictions, within the power and control of the legislature.

Appointment, in the broad sense of being chosen, selected, or designated to occupy the position of teacher, principal, or superintendent, by the proper authorities in accordance with all statutory requirements, is generally a prerequisite to employment in such capacity.[63] The matter of appointment of such school employees is, subject to constitutional restrictions, within the power and control of the legislature.[64] The usual rules of statutory construction govern the construction of statutes relating to the appointment of teachers and other instructional employees.[65]

50. Neb.—State v. Grosvenor, 27 N.W. 728, 19 Neb. 494.

51. Neb.—State v. Grosvenor, supra.

52. Kan.—Strange v. School Dist. No. 97, 295 P. 672, 132 Kan. 268.
Tenn.—**Corpus Juris quoted in** State ex rel. Clement v. Dodson, 83 S.W.2d 558, 169 Tenn. 178.
Wyo.—**Corpus Juris quoted in** State ex rel. Pape v. Hockett, 156 P.2d 299, 305, 61 Wyo. 145.
56 C.J. p 377 note 4.

53. Tenn.—**Corpus Juris quoted in** State ex rel. Clement v. Dodson, 83 S.W.2d 558, 169 Tenn. 178.
Wyo.—**Corpus Juris quoted in** State ex rel. Pape v. Hockett, 156 P.2d 299, 305, 61 Wyo. 145.
56 C.J. p 377 note 5.

54. Tenn.—**Corpus Juris quoted in** State ex rel. Clement v. Dodson, 83 S.W.2d 558, 169 Tenn. 178.
Wyo.—**Corpus Juris quoted in** State ex rel. Pape v. Hockett, 156 P.2d 299, 305, 61 Wyo. 145.
56 C.J. p 377 note 6.

55. Tenn.—**Corpus Juris quoted in** State ex rel. Clement v. Dodson, 83 S.W.2d 558, 169 Tenn. 178.
Wyo.—**Corpus Juris quoted in** State ex rel. Pape v. Hockett, 156 P.2d 299, 305, 61 Wyo. 145.
56 C.J. p 377 note 7.

56. Tenn.—**Corpus Juris quoted in** State ex rel. Clement v. Dodson, 83 S.W.2d 558, 169 Tenn. 178.
Wis.—Clune v. Buchanan School Dist. No. 3, 166 N.W. 11, 166 Wis. 452, 6 A.L.R. 736.

57. N.D.—McDonald v. Nielson, 175 N.W. 361, 43 N.D. 346.
Tenn.—**Corpus Juris quoted in** State ex rel. Clement v. Dodson, 83 S.W.2d 558. 169 Tenn. 178.
Wyo.—**Corpus Juris quoted in** State ex rel. Pape v. Hockett, 156 P.2d 299, 305, 61 Wyo. 145.

58. N.D.—Wendt v. Waller, 176 N.W. 930, 46 N.D. 268.
Tenn.—**Corpus Juris quoted in** State ex rel. Clement v. Dodson, 83 S.W.2d 558, 169 Tenn. 178.
Wyo.—**Corpus Juris quoted in** State ex rel. Pape v. Hockett, 156 P.2d 299, 305, 61 Wyo. 145.

59. W.Va.—Capehart v. Graham Dist. Board of Education, 95 S.E. 838, 82 W.Va. 217.
Revocation of certificate for failure to attend see supra § 165.

60. W.Va.—Capehart v. Graham Dist. Board of Education, supra.

61. W.Va.—Capehart v. Graham Dist. Board of Education, supra.

62. Mich.—Hammond v. Muskegon School Board, 67 N.W. 973, 109 Mich. 676.

63. N.J.—Moriarity v. Board of Education of City of Garfield in Bergen County, 42 A.2d 465, 133 N.J. Law 73, affirmed 46 A.2d 734, 134 N.J.Law 356.
N.Y.—Nicol v. New York City Board of Education, 211 N.Y.S. 749, 125 Misc. 678.
Pa.—Potts v. School Dist. of Penn. Tp., 193 A. 290, 127 Pa.Super. 173.
W.Va.—Rowan v. Board of Education of Logan County, 24 S.E.2d 583, 125 W.Va. 406.
Contracts of employment see infra §§ 183-187.

64. Ill.—Groves v. Board of Education of Chicago, 10 N.E.2d 403, 367 Ill. 91 appeal dismissed 58 S.Ct. 746, 303 U.S. 122, 82 L.Ed. 1085, rehearing denied 58 S.Ct. 763, 303 U.S. 669, 82 L.Ed. 1125.

65. **Statutes construed**
(1) Statute conferring power to appoint a superintendent of schools

78 C.J.S.—63

993

Exhibit 5. Photostatic copy of page 993 in Volume 78 of *Corpus Juris Secundum*. Reproduced with permission of the publisher and copyright owner, The American Law Book Company, Brooklyn, N. Y.

F. Teachers, Principals, and Superintendents, secs. 154-238.
   1. *In General,* secs. 154-169.
   2. *Selection, Appointment, or Election,* secs. 170-182.
   3. *Contracts of Employment,* secs. 183-197.
   4. *Assignment and Transfer,* secs. 198-199.
   5. *Change of Status,* secs. 200-217.
   6. *Compensation, Board and Lodging, and Pensions,* secs. 218-236.
   7. *Duties and Liabilities,* secs. 237-238.

G. Property, Contracts, and Liabilities, secs. 239-322.

H. Fiscal Management, Debts, Securities, and Taxation, secs. 323-413.

I. Remedies of Taxpayers in General, secs. 414-422.

J. Presentation and Allowance of Claims, secs. 423-427.

K. Actions, secs. 428-444.

L. Pupils, and Conduct and Discipline of Schools, secs. 445-508.
   1. *Admission and Attendance of Pupils,* secs. 445-482.
   2. *School Terms, Classification of Pupils, and Instruction,* secs. 483-492.
   3. *Control of Pupils and Discipline,* secs. 493-505.
   4. *Graduation, Scholarships, and Diplomas,* secs. 506-508.

M. Miscellaneous Criminal Offences, secs. 509-512.

The sections under each of these major topics are outlined with considerable detail. In the body of the volume, each subtopic is discussed as is exemplified in Exhibit 5. The pocket parts which keep *Corpus Juris Secundum* up to date show subsequent cases according to the footnote numbers in the bound volume.

Study of Exhibit 5 together with the outline reproduced in part should indicate the type of information available in *Corpus Juris Secundum.* Footnotes in *Corpus Juris* (the first edition) are not repeated in *Corpus Juris Secundum* and the original edition will not be completely superseded for historical studies.

American Jurisprudence 2d. American Jurisprudence 2d is a complete revision and rewriting of the original edition, *American Jurisprudence* and its predecessor, *Ruling Case Law.* It is encyclopedic in style similar to both editions of *Corpus Juris* but it contains only the leading cases whereas *Corpus Juris* and *Corpus Juris Secundum* are all inclusive. *Since* American Jurisprudence 2d *is in the process of being published and only 34 volumes of the estimated 70-volume set are released, the researcher in school law must rely on* American Jurisprudence *since the subject "schools" is included in a future volume.*

Following is an outline of the topics included in *American Juris-*

one is not justified in relying upon representations relating to facts of which he has a better knowledge than the party making the representations[14] is likewise applicable to contracts of this nature.[15]

Where, by statute, an oath of allegiance to the Federal and state Constitutions and of fidelity to duty is required to be embodied in a teacher's contract of employment, the oath will be deemed to have been embodied in the contract where it was administered on the occasion and at the time when the contract was executed, and a statement subscribed by the teacher, embodying the oath, is found below the signature of the parties to the contract.[16]

§ 116. —With School Board Member or Wife of Member.—In agreement with the elementary principle that a member of a school board may not enter into a contract with the board in which he has a personal interest,[17] a school board cannot contract with one of its own members to teach the school.[18] But in jurisdictions where the earnings of the wife are her separate property, a school board may contract to employ the wife of a member as a teacher,[19] although in states where the earnings of the wife constitute part of the community property of which the husband has the control and management,[20] the decisions are to the contrary.[1]

§ 117. —Extending beyond Term of Board; Contracts Beginning in Subsequent Term.—In contrast with the general rule applicable to contracts by

year, were informed by the superintendent of schools that the school budget did not admit of their paying the amount of salary named in the contract were precluded by their delay from rescinding the contract because of the principal's misrepresentation as to the amount of the budget, even if otherwise entitled to rely on such misrepresentations as a fraud justifying the rescission, where, for over two months, they did nothing to repudiate the contract, but permitted the principal to prepare for the school term, and finally to enter upon his duties when school opened on August 30, the notice terminating the contract not having been served upon him until September 20, it being then too late to secure another position. Weir v. School Dist. 200 Wash 172, 93 P(2d) 308, 123 ALR 1057.

14 See 23 Am Jur 947, Fraud and Deceit, § 146.

15 Weir v. School Dist. 200 Wash 172, 93 P(2d) 308, 123 ALR 1057.

School directors were not justified in relying upon misrepresentations by one whom they employed as principal, that he had consulted the county superintendent and was advised by her that the school budget had been approved and that the district would be able to pay him the amount named in the contract, upon which misrepresentations they predicated fraud as justification for termination of the contract, where they were themselves the persons who tentatively were to determine and express the needs and abilities of the district, and they knew that the approval of the budget lay with the county superintendent and the reviewing board and were told repeatedly by the superintendent that they would not have money enough to pay so large a salary as that named in the contract. Ibid.

16 June v. School Dist. 283 Mich 533, 278 NW 676, 116 ALR 581 (stating further that such a requirement will be given a reasonable construction).

The lack of a jurat to such an oath does not render the employment contract fatally defective so as to preclude its enforcement. June v. School Dist. 283 Mich 533, 278 NW 676, 116 ALR 581. Anno: 116 ALR 587.

17 See supra, § 49.

18 Scott v. School Dist. 67 Vt 150, 31 A 145, 27 LRA 588.

The reason for the rule is clearer when it is considered that it is the duty of the board to remove a teacher when necessary; it is fundamental that a man shall not be a judge in his own case. Ibid.

The inclusion, however, by a county superintendent of schools of his own name in a list of approved teachers of the county does not invalidate a subsequent contract employing him as a teacher, where the superintendent does not himself employ the teachers but merely submits a list of names to the board of education, which is the employing authority. White v. Board of Education, 117 W Va 114, 184 SE 264, 103 ALR 1376.

19 Thompson v. School Dist. 252 Mich 629, 233 NW 439, 74 ALR 790.

Anno: 74 ALR 792.

A contract employing as a teacher the wife of a school board member whose concurrence is necessary in order to bind the district is not within the meaning of a statute declaring it to be illegal for any member of a board of education "to be personally interested in any way, directly or indirectly, in any contract with the district in which he holds office," where the earnings of a married woman are her separate property. Thompson v. School Dist. 252 Mich 629, 233 NW 439, 74 ALR 790.

20 See 11 Am Jur 196, Community Property, § 34.

1 Anno: 74 ALR 795.

Exhibit 6. Photostatic copy of page 378 in Volume 47 of *American Jurisprudence*. Reproduced with permission of the publishers and copyright owners, The Lawyers Co-operative Publishing Company, Rochester, N.Y., and Bancroft-Whitney Company, San Francisco, Calif.

prudence.[7] Not only may this outline be compared with the outline of *Corpus Juris Secundum*, previously shown; the actual material in the two encyclopedias may also be compared. Exhibit 6 shows a page from *American Jurisprudence* and Exhibit 5 showed a page from *Corpus Juris Secundum.*

I. INTRODUCTORY. (1-11).
II. SCHOOL DISTRICTS. (12-28).
III. ADMINISTRATIVE OFFICERS AND BOARDS. (29-47).
IV. CONTRACTS IN GENERAL. (48-55).
V. TORT LIABILITY. (56-61).
VI. SCHOOL PROPERTY AND BUILDINGS. (62-75).
VII. TAXATION. (76-82).
VIII. SCHOOL FUNDS AND EXPENDITURES. (83-107).
IX. TEACHERS AND OTHER EMPLOYEES. (108-145).
  A. In General. (108-113).
  B. Employment and Compensation in General. (114-126).
  C. Teachers' Tenure Statutes. (127-145).
X. PUPILS; ADMISSION, ATTENDANCE, DISCIPLINE, AND PUNISHMENT. (146-188).
  A. In General. (146-150).
  B. Right to Attend Schools. (151-155).
  C. Compulsory Attendance. (156-159).
  D. Transportation of Pupils. (160-166).
  E. Disciplinary Regulations. (167-172).
  F. Discipline and Punishment. (173-188).
XI. HEALTH REGULATIONS. (189-199).
XII. COURSES OF INSTRUCTION, TEXTBOOKS, AND SUPPLIES. (200-207).
XIII. SECTARIANISM IN SCHOOLS. (208-215).
XIV. RACE SEGREGATION. (216-219).
XV. PRIVATE SCHOOLS. (220-229).

Corpus Juris Secundum and *American Jurisprudence* both use the same style of presentation: textual material with copious footnotes giving citations to cases illustrating the statements of principles in the text on the upper part of the page. The chief difference between them is in the scope of material included. Most topics are more extensively treated in *Corpus Juris Secundum* than in *American Jurisprudence.*

---

[7] Reproduced with permission of the publishers and copyright owners, The Lawyers Co-operative Publishing Company, Rochester, N. Y., and Bancroft-Whitney Company, San Francisco, Calif.

However, for the purpose of research in school-law problems, *American Jurisprudence* may be adequate coverage. Choice between these two encyclopedias will depend upon the purpose of the investigator's study. If an exhaustive piece of research is contemplated, *Corpus Juris Secundum* will provide a greater fund of information than *American Jurisprudence*. On the other hand, *American Jurisprudence* is sufficient for most research in school law by school administrators, teachers, or others who are not concerned with technical niceties and distinctions of interest to lawyers.

Summary

Many lawyers are of the opinion that one without legal training should not touch a law book. They are as jealous of their prerogatives as a physician of his instruments, and rightly so. This appendix has been included in this text because students of education have attempted to search legal problems affecting the public schools in connection with graduate study requirements. In so doing they have on occasion used secondary sources which are possibly unreliable or antiquated; they have quoted statutes that have been repealed or possibly declared unconstitutional; they have cited court decisions which have been overruled. It is safer to instruct a layman how to use technical instruments than to leave them unguarded for indiscriminate use by the zealous but untaught. If students of education are to learn school law, they should know how to find it.

PLACE A STRAIGHTEDGE ALONG THIS LINE AND TEAR OUT

Chapter II

EXERCISES ON THE USE OF THE LAW LIBRARY

■ Section A—STATE COURT DECISIONS

1. Name the official and unofficial reports for your state.

What courts do they cover?

2. Does your state have a digest or digests?
   a. Yes No
   b. State the exact title or titles?

   c. What purpose does the state digest serve?

3. **Name the component parts of the National Reporter System.**

PLACE A STRAIGHTEDGE ALONG THIS LINE AND TEAR OUT

4. What National Reporter is used for your state?

5. What states have their decisions published in the National Reporter covering your state?

6. What is the purpose of the National Reporter Blue Book?

7. Is there a digest for your region?
   a. Yes No
   b. What is the exact title of the regional digest?

c. What purpose does the regional digest serve?

8. Refer to the National Reporter System and the National Reporter Blue Book and locate the following cases in the various reporters. Give the name of the case, regional citation (to show the parallel citation for each), and the date of the case.

Example:

77 Utah 270	*Tuttle et al.* v. *Board of Education,* 294 P. 294 (1930).
a. 230 Ala. 401	a.
b. 263 Ill. 536	b.
c. 109 Ark. 125	c.
d. 61 Mich. 299	d.
e. 123 Iowa 55	e.
f. 64 N. H. 303	f.

PLACE A STRAIGHTEDGE ALONG THIS LINE AND TEAR OUT

g. 186 Wash. 684 g.

h. 153 Mass. 426 h.

i. 145 Ohio St. 243 i.

j. 169 Wis. 231 j.

9. Refer to the National Reporter System and, if necessary, to the table of cases of the particular regional reporter and locate the following cases in the various reporters. Give the name of the case, state citation (to show the parallel citation for each), and the date of the case.

Example:

108 So. 588 — *Phoenix City* v. *County Board of Education*, 214 Ala. 620 (1926).

a. 284 S.W. 764 a.

b. 169 P. 314 b.

c. 130 S.W. 1105 c.

d. 106 P. 578	d.
e. 46 N.W. 528	e.
f. 125 So. 841	f.
g. 30 A. (2d) 779	g.
h. 166 N.W. 820	h.
i. 28 P. (2d) 455	i.
j. 88 S.E. 256	j.

PLACE A STRAIGHTEDGE ALONG THIS LINE AND TEAR OUT

■ Section B—STATE AND FEDERAL INFORMATION

1. What part of the Constitution of the United States of America refers to education?

2. What reference regarding education, if any, is made in your state constitution?

3. Does your state publish a "School Code"?

   a. What is the *exact* title of it?

   b. Who publishes it?

   c. How does one receive a copy of it?

   d. Is it considered an official legal reference in your state?

4. Does your State Department of Public Instruction publish summaries of current legislation, regular comments on current court decisions, and/or comments on current attorney general's opinions?

   a. List the exact titles of any such publications which are current.

5. Does your state publish the opinions of the attorney general?
   a. Yes No

6. Does the publication report all opinions or are the opinions published selected to be illustrative of an opinion rendered more than once on a similar question of law?
   a. Inclusive Selective

7. How would you use the publication of attorney generals' opinions to research a topic? Be specific.

PLACE A STRAIGHTEDGE ALONG THIS LINE AND TEAR OUT

■ Section C—AMERICAN DIGEST SYSTEM

This system covers all cases in all states, and it provides digests of each case key-numbered by topics. The system is arranged by decennial editions, with the exception of the first and current publications.

1. List the titles and dates of the publications included in the American Digest System.

Title *Date*

2. Find "Schools and School Districts" in the sixth Decennial Digest.

a. What is the general heading of Key #82?

b. Locate Key #82(1) and do the following:

(1). How many cases are listed under Tennessee?

(2). What is the summary of the case or cases?

(3). Give the complete citation including the date of the case or cases.

PLACE A STRAIGHTEDGE ALONG THIS LINE AND TEAR OUT

■ Section D—ENCYCLOPEDIAS AND ANNOTATIONS

Corpus Juris Secundum

1. In what volume or volumes is the subject "Schools and School Districts" covered?

2. What is the general heading of Section 115?

3. What is the general rule governing Section 115?

4. Give the complete citation for footnote #78 (include the date).

American Jurisprudence

1. In what volume or volumes is the subject "Schools" covered?

2. What is the general heading of Section 95?

3. What is the general rule governing Section 95?

4. What was the issue in *Nohl* v. *Board of Education?*

PLACE A STRAIGHTEDGE ALONG THIS LINE AND TEAR OUT

American Law Reports

Using A.L.R. Annotated, locate the section on "Schools" and do the following:

1. What is the title of Section 42?

2. What reference is given to *American Jurisprudence?*

3. Give the complete citation of the first case listed under Section 42.

4. What editions must be used to obtain a complete reference to A.L.R. citations?

5. **In what edition is the last reference made to Section 42? Give the complete citation to the case cited.**

6. **What is the issue in the case listed under No. 5?**

State Encyclopedias

1. Is an encyclopedia published for your state?
   a. Yes No

2. What is the exact title of the encyclopedia?

PLACE A STRAIGHTEDGE ALONG THIS LINE AND TEAR OUT

■ Section E—INDEX TO LEGAL PERIODICALS

Note: For reference use the September 1959-August 1960 cumulative issue of the index.

1. *Periodicals Index*

   Does the index cover the following magazines? (Circle answer.)

Yes	No	*Catholic Lawyer*
Yes	No	*Wisconsin Law Review*
Yes	No	*Brooklyn Law Review*
Yes	No	*Detroit Legal News*
Yes	No	*Shingle*

2. *Subject Index*

   An article was written on high school drop-outs and corrective measures. Give the complete citation. Do not abbreviate the title of the publication.

3. *Author Index*

   Clark Byse wrote an article on academic freedom. Give the complete citation.

4. *Book Review Index*

Who reviewed *Tenure in American Higher Education* by Clark Byse and Louis Joughin? Give the complete citation.

5. *Cases Commented Upon*

What reviews contain comments on the case of *Molitor* v. *Kaneland Community Unit District (Ill.)*, 163 N.E. (2d) 89?

PLACE A STRAIGHTEDGE ALONG THIS LINE AND TEAR OUT

■ Section F—STATE DIGESTS

Refer to the digest of your state, if your state has a digest, to answer the following questions. Give the citation to a case in point and the topic and section of the digest. If the digest does not comment on any one of the following four topics, indicate this fact with a brief statement.

1. Is corporal punishment permitted?

2. May the local school district provide transportation to private and parochial schools?

3. May state aid be distributed to private and parochial schools?

4. Is the local school district required to meet all local zoning ordinances and regulations?

5. Is collective bargaining established by law in your state?
   a. Yes No

   b. What is the statutory citation?

PLACE A STRAIGHTEDGE ALONG THIS LINE AND TEAR OUT

■ Section G—USE OF SHEPARD'S CITATIONS TO CASES

Part 1 refers to decisions by state courts; Part 2 to a decision by the Supreme Court of the United States.

Part 1

State Courts

Select *one* of the following cases, whichever is in your region:

28 N.W. 105

24 A.(2d) 468

50 P.(2d) 36

135 N.E. 459

70 So. 557

86 S.E. 545

191 S.W. 781

1. What is the name of the case?

2. In what state was the case originally decided?

3. In what year was it decided?

4. Shepardize the case.

PLACE A STRAIGHTEDGE ALONG THIS LINE AND TEAR OUT

5. Is the case still controlling?

6. What is the latest citation? Include the name of the case, citation, and the date.

Part 2

The Supreme Court of the United States

1. What is the name of the case found at 281 U. S. 370?

2. In what state was the case originally decided?

3. What action was taken by the Supreme Court of the United States?

4. Has the decision of the U. S. Supreme Court been cited by the courts of states? Name the states.

5. Shepardize the case. (Use Shepard's United States Citations.)

6. Is the case still controlling?

7. What is the latest citation? Include the name of the case, citation, and the date.

Chapter III

ANALYSIS OF A CASE*

■ EDUCATION AS A STATE FUNCTION—POWER OF THE STATE OVER ITS SCHOOL SYSTEM—UNIFORM TEXTBOOK LEGISLATION

State ex rel. *Clark et al.* v. *Halworth, Trustee*
122 Ind. 462, 23 N.E. 946, 7 L.R.A. 240 (1890)

I. Summary of essential facts:

A. The Indiana legislature passed an act which

1. provided for a uniform series of textbooks to be used in all public schools of the state, and

2. provided that the exclusive right to sell such textbooks be awarded to the lowest and best bidder.

B. The school trustee of Monroe Township, Howard County, refused to certify to the county superintendent the number of books that would be required.

C. A writ of mandamus was sought to compel the trustee to present such a certified statement.

*An acceptable analysis submitted by a graduate student enrolled in the "Legal Aspects of School Administration" at The University of Wisconsin-Milwaukee.

D. The petition for the writ of mandamus was contested on the grounds that the statute was unconstitutional as

1. impinging upon the right of local self-government, and
2. creating a monopoly in favor of the successful bidder.

E. The lower court held the act unconstitutional.

F. Upon appeal to the Supreme Court, it was ruled that the act was constitutional.

II. Definition of the major issues in dispute:

A. What is the extent of the power of the state over its school system?

B. May the state award contracts for the purchase of textbooks even when such an awarding will bring benefit to a private person?

III. Significant legal principles set forth in the decision:

A. The schools in which are educated and trained the children who are to become the rulers of the Commonwealth are matters of state and not of local jurisdiction.

B. It is for the law-making power to determine whether the authority shall be exercised by a state board of education or distributed to county, township, or city organizations throughout the state.

C. The governing school boards derive all their authority from the statute and can exercise no powers except those expressly granted and those which result by necessary implication from the grant.

D. As the power over schools is legislative, it is not exhausted by exercise. To deny the power to change is to affirm that progress is impossible.

E. It is impossible to conceive of the existence of a uniform system of common schools without power lodged somewhere to make it uniform . . . and that power must necessarily reside in the legislature; such power must include the authority to prescribe the course of study, the system of instruction, and the books which shall be used.

F. The legislature has authority to impose upon all officers whose tenures are legislative such duties respecting school affairs as it deems proper.

G. The effect of the statute is not to make officers perform duties for the benefit of private individuals but for the benefit of the public, and that benefit results to private persons is an unavoidable incident, not a designed or express provision of the statute. At the time the act was passed, it was not known nor could it be known what persons would secure the contract, for it provided that competition should be invited and the contract awarded to the lowest bidder.

IV. I consider the decision to be sound here in terms of good educational policy.

A. Subject only to such restrictions as are contained in the state or United States constitutions, the legislatures have plenary power in educational matters in the states.

B. By inference, all activities of a local board of trustees are state rather than local activities.

C. The fact that a monopoly was created was incidental and unavoidable.

Chapter IV

GLOSSARY OF LEGAL TERMS*

Action. An ordinary proceeding in a court by which one party prosecutes another for the enforcement or protection of a right, the redress of a wrong, or the punishment of a public offense. In common language, a "suit," or "lawsuit."

Action at law. Court action in a law case, as distinguished from equity.

Actionable. That which furnishes legal grounds for an action. Sometimes a court will say "The action will lie," meaning that the circumstances are such that there is a ground for court action.

Ad litum. Latin, meaning for the purpose of the suit, usually used when minors are, in fact, the plaintiffs. Because they are minors they must sue "by next friend," referring to parent or guardian who is plaintiff for the purpose of the suit.

Allegation. Statement in pleadings, setting forth what the party expects to prove.

Allege. To state, assert, or charge; to make an allegation.

Amicus curiae. "Friend at court"—one who volunteers or is requested to give information to the court regarding some matter of law in regard to which the judge is doubtful or mistaken; one who has no right to appear in a case but is allowed to file a brief or enter into the argument because of an indirect interest.

Annotation. Notes or commentaries in addition to the principal text. A book is said to be annotated when it contains such notes.

Appellant. The party who takes an appeal from one court to another.

Appellee. The party against whom an appeal is taken.

Arbitrary. Not supported by fair cause and without reason given.

Arbitration. Submission of a controversy, usually in labor disputes, for determination. *See* Mediation.

Assault. An attempt to beat another, without touching him. *See* Battery.

Attractive nuisance. A condition, instrumentality, machine, or other agency, dangerous to young children because of their inability to appreciate its danger because they may be expected to be attracted to it. *See* Nuisance.

Avoid a contract. To cancel and make the contract void.

---

*Reproduced from *School Law* by Madaline Kinter Remmlein, Danville, Illinois: The Interstate Printers & Publishers, Inc., 1962.

Battery. An unlawful beating or other wrongful physical violence inflicted on another without his consent. The offer or attempt to commit a battery is an assault. There can be an assault without a battery; battery always includes assault. The two words are usually used together.

Bill. A written complaint filed in a court.

Bill of attainder. An act of the legislature inflicting a penalty (technically capital punishment) without conviction in judicial proceedings. Loosely used to include all legislation imposing a penalty applicable to acts not considered a crime when committed.

Breach of contract. Failure without legal excuse to perform part or the whole of a contract.

Certificate. A document designed as notice that some act has been done, or some event occurred, or some legal formality complied with; evidence of qualification.

Citations. References to law books. A citation includes the book where the reference is found, the volume number, and section or page numbers. A uniform system of abbreviations in case law has been adopted, but statutory materials differ from state to state according to the official designation accepted by the legislature.

Citations, judicial. References to court decisions. Citations in the case materials in this text refer to official state reports and to the National Reporter System. The volume number precedes the abbreviation of the reporter, and the page number follows it. In parentheses is the name of the state where the decision was rendered, and its date. A complete judicial citation includes everywhere that the case may be found, but for school-law work complete parallel citations are unnecessary.

Citations, statutory. References to statutes; where the statute may be found in publicly available form. Statutory citations in this text include the name of the volume, the title and/or chapter, and the section number(s) quoted.

Civil action. One brought to recover some civil right, or to obtain redress for some wrong.

Class bill or suit. A case in which one or more in a numerous class, having a common interest in the issue, sue in behalf of themselves and all others of the class.

Closed shop. Term in labor law meaning that worker must be a member of the union as a condition precedent to employment. *See* Union shop.

Code. A compilation of statutes, scientifically arranged into chapters, subheadings, and sections, with a table of contents and index.

Codification. Process of collecting and arranging the laws of a state into a code.

Collateral attack. An attempt to destroy the effect of a judgment by reopening the merits of a case or by showing reasons why the judgment should not have been given, in an action other than that in which the judgment was given; that is, not in an appeal.

Common Law. As used in this text, legal principles derived from usage and custom, or from court decisions affirming such usages and customs, or the acts of Parliament in force at the time of the American Revolution, as distinguished from law created by enactment of American legislatures.

Concurrent jurisdiction. Two courts having the same authority.

Concurring opinion. An opinion written by a judge who agrees with the majority of the court as to the decision in a case, but has different reasons for arriving at that decision.

Consideration in contracts. The inducement, usually an amount of money.

Constitution. The supreme organic and fundamental law of a nation or state, establishing the character and conception of its government, laying the basic principles to which its internal life is to be conformed, organizing the government, and regulating, distributing, and limiting the functions of its different departments, and prescribing the extent and manner of the exercise of sovereign powers.

Contract. An agreement upon sufficient consideration, to do or not to do a particular thing; the writing which contains the agreement of the parties, with the terms and conditions, and which serves as proof of the obligation.

Contract action. An action brought to enforce rights under a contract.

Credibility of witnesses. Worthiness of belief of testimony of witnesses.

Criminal action. Proceeding by which a party charged with a crime is brought to trial and punishment.

Damages. Pecuniary compensation or indemnity which may be recovered in court by the person who has suffered loss or injury to his person, property, or rights through the unlawful act, or omission, or negligence of another.

De facto officer. One who is in actual possession of an office without lawful title; as opposed to a *de jure* officer.

De jure officer. One who has just claim and rightful title to an office, although not necessarily in actual possession thereof.

Declaratory relief. A judgment which declares the rights of the parties or expresses the opinion of the court on a question of law, without ordering anything to be done.

Decree. Order of court of equity announcing the legal consequences of the facts found.

Defendant. The party against whom relief or recovery is sought in a court action.

Defendant in error. Defendant in appellate court when the "appeal" is for review on writ of error.

Defense. That which is offered and alleged by the defendant as a reason in law or fact why the plaintiff should not recover.

Demurrer. Allegation by one party that other party's allegations may be true but, even so, are not of such legal consequence as to justify proceeding with the case.

Dictum. Statement of a legal principle by a court, which principle is not necessitated by the facts or the law of the case; because such statements are not directly in point, they are not controlling precedents, though often persuasive.

Directory. An instruction of no obligatory force and involving no invalidating consequences for its disregard.

Dismissed for want of equity. Case dismissed because the allegations in the complaint have been found untrue, or because they are insufficient to entitle complainant to the relief sought.

Dissenting opinion. The opinion in which a judge announces his dissent from the conclusions held by the majority of the court.

Divisible contract. One which can be separated into two or more parts not necessarily dependent on each other nor intended by the parties to be so.

Discrimination, unconstitutional. The effect of a statute which confers particular privileges on a class arbitrarily selected and for whom no reasonable distinction can be found.

Due process. The exercise of the powers of government in such a way as to protect individual rights.

Ejusdem generis. Of the same kind, class, or nature. In statutory construction the *ejusdem generis* rule is that, where general words follow an enumeration of words of a particular and specific meaning, the general words are not interpreted in their widest sense but as applying to persons or things of the same general kind or class as those specifically mentioned.

Emancipation of child. Surrender of the right to care, custody, and earnings of a child by its parents who at the same time renounce parental duties.

Enforceable contract. Any contract not void or voidable because defective.

Enjoin. To require a person, by writ of injunction from a court of equity, to perform, or to abstain or desist from, some act.

Equitable relief. Decree in court of equity.

Equity. As used in this text, the field of jurisprudence differing in origin, theory, and methods from the common law.

Estop. To prevent.

Estoppel. A bar raised by the law which prevents a man from alleging or denying a certain fact because of his previous statements or conduct.

Ex post facto. After the fact. An ex post facto law is one passed after an act which retrospectively changes the legal consequences of that act. The Federal Constitution prohibits the passage of ex post facto laws, referring to criminal laws only. *See* Bill of attainder and Retroactive.

Ex rel. Abbreviation for *ex relatione*, meaning on relation or information. For the purpose of this text, it need be explained only as designating a type of court action.

Exception. In civil procedure, a formal objection to the action of the court when it refuses a request or overrules an objection, implying that the party excepting does not acquiesce in the court's ruling and may base an appeal thereon.

Executed contract. A completed contract as opposed to one which is executory.

Executory contract. An incompletely performed contract; something yet to be done in the future.

Governmental immunity. Immunity from tort actions enjoyed by governmental units in common-law states.

Hearing on the merits. Trial on the substance of a case as opposed to consideration of procedure only.

Hearsay evidence. Testimony given by a witness who relates what others have told him or what he has heard said by others, rather than what he knows personally.

In loco parentis. In place of the parent; charged with some of the parents' rights, duties, and responsibilities.

In re. Concerning. When used in a title of a court case, it merely designates a type of case.

Indivisible contract. One which forms a whole, the performance of every part a condition precedent to bind the other party; as opposed to a divisible contract which is composed of independent parts the performance of any one of which will bind the other party only as far as it goes.

Information. An accusation against a person.

Infringement. An encroachment upon or invasion of one's rights.

Injunction. A prohibitive writ issued by a court of equity forbidding the defendant to do some act he is threatening, or forbidding him to continue doing some act which is injurious to the plaintiff and cannot be adequately redressed by an action at law.

Injunction, temporary. An injunction granted at the beginning of a suit to restrain the defendant from doing some act, the right to which is in dispute, and which may be discharged or made permanent according to the result of the case after the rights of the parties are determined.

Invalid. Not binding; lacking in authority.

Ipso facto. By the fact itself.

Judgment. Decision of the court, usually that part involving the payment of damages.

Judgment-proof. Said of those against whom a judgment has been rendered even though they are not in financial condition to pay it.

Laches. Omission to assert a right for an unreasonable and unexplained length of time, under circumstances prejudicial to the adverse party.

Law. (1) System of principles or rules of human conduct. In this sense it includes decisions of courts as well as acts of legislatures. (2) An enactment of a legislature, a statute.

Legal disability. Lack of legal capacity to perform an act.

Legal power. The right or ability to do some act.

Liability. Legal responsibility.

Liquidated damages. A specific sum of money stipulated by the parties by bond or contract as the amount of damages to be recovered by one party for breach of the agreement by the other.

Majority opinion. The statement of reasons for the views of the majority of the members of the bench in a decision in which some of them disagree.

Majority rule. A legal principle upheld by the majority of decisions on the question, when there is a lesser number of decisions to the contrary on the same issue.

Malfeasance. Commission of an unlawful act, applied to public officers and employees. *See* Misfeasance and Nonfeasance.

Mandamus. A writ to compel a public body or its officers to perform a duty.

Mandatory. Compulsory, referring to a command for which disregard or disobedience is unlawful.

Mediation. Attempt to reconcile differences, usually in labor disputes. *See* Arbitration.

Minority rule. The principle upheld by some courts on an issue which has been decided to the contrary by the majority of courts.

Misdemeanor. An offense lower than a felony and usually punishable by fine, or imprisonment otherwise than in a penitentiary.

Misfeasance. Improper performance of a lawful act. *See* Malfeasance.

Nonfeasance. Omission to perform a required duty.

Nolens volens. With or without consent.

Nonsuit. Judgment against a plaintiff when he is unable to prove a case, or when he neglects to proceed to the trial of a case after it has been put in issue.

Nuisance. A continuous condition or use of property in such a manner as to obstruct proper use of it by others lawfully having right to use it, or the public.

Parol-evidence rule. Oral evidence as to matters not contained in a written contract or other instrument is not admissible.

Persuasive value. Influence of decisions of one jurisdiction in another jurisdiction.

Petition. Written application or prayer to the court for the redress of a wrong or the grant of a privilege or license.

Petitioner. The one who presents a petition to the court; same as plaintiff in other kinds of cases.

Plaintiff. Person who brings an action; he who sues by filing a complaint.

Plea in abatement. An objection to the place, method, or time of plaintiff's assertion of a claim, without disputing the justice of the claim.

Pleadings. Formal papers filed in court action including complaint by plaintiff and defendant's answer, showing what is alleged on one side and admitted or denied on the other side.

Plenary. Complete power, usually applied to legislatures over matters within their entire jurisdiction; applicable also to any public officer who has unqualified power in a designated matter.

Police power. As used in this text, legislative power to enact laws for the comfort, health, and prosperity of the state; for the general welfare of the people concerned.

Power. The authority to do something expressly or impliedly granted.

Prayer. The part of the petition in which petitioner requests the court to grant the relief sought.

Precedent. A decision considered as furnishing an example or authority for an identical or similar case afterward arising on a similar question of law.

Prima facie case. A case in which the evidence is so strong that the adverse party can overthrow the evidence only by sufficient rebutting evidence.

Privies of parties. Persons connected with mutual interest in the same action.

Quantum meruit. An implication that the defendant had promised to pay plaintiff as much as he reasonably deserved for work or labor.

Quasi-. As if, or almost as if it were, *e.g.*, quasi-judicial act of a school board in holding a hearing before dismissal of a teacher.

Quo warranto—information in the nature of a quo warranto. Method of trying title to a public office.

Ratification. Confirmation of a transaction by one who before ratification had the optional right to relieve himself of its obligation.

Regulations. Rules for management or government.

Relator. One on whose complaint certain writs are issued; for all practical purposes, the plaintiff.

Relief. The redress or assistance which a complainant seeks from the court; not properly applied to money damages.

Remand a case. To send the case back to the court from which it came for further proceedings there, after an appellate decision.

Res adjudicata. A matter judicially decided.

Rescission of contract. Cancellation or abrogation by the parties, or one of them.

Respondent. Defendant in certain kinds of cases.

Restrain. To prohibit from action; to enjoin.

Retroactive. A law which creates a new obligation on considerations already past, or destroys or impairs former privileges. Not all retroactive laws are unconstitutional.

Right. A power or privilege in one person against another.

Scienter. Knowingly; defendant knew the circumstances leading to his injury. Used chiefly in loyalty laws.

Stare decisis. Principle that when a court has made a declaration of a legal principle it is the law until changed by competent authority; upholding of precedents within the jurisdiction.

Statute. Act of the legislature.

Stipulation. (1) A particular provision in an agreement; (2) an agreement between counsel concerning business before a court.

Subpoena. Process commanding a witness to appear and testify.

Sufficiency of evidence. Evidence adequate in character, weight, or amount to justify legal action sought.

Tenure. In its general sense, mode of holding an office or position, especially with respect to time.

Tort. Legal wrong committed upon the person, reputation, or property of another, independent of contract.

Ultra vires. Acts beyond the scope of authority.

Union shop. Term in labor law meaning that, although nonmembers of the union may be employed, they must join the union within a designated time or face dismissal.

Validity. Legal sufficiency in contradistinction to mere regularity.

Vested right. A right which has so completely and definitely accrued or settled in a person that it cannot be cancelled or impaired.

Void. Ineffectual, having no legal force or binding effect; said of a contract so defective that nothing can cure it.

Voidable. That which may be avoided or declared void; as to contracts, a defective instrument which can be cured by ratification by the one who could have avoided it.

Waive. To renounce or abandon a right.

Waiver. Intentional and voluntary relinquishment of a known right.

Without prejudice. No rights or privileges will be considered waived or lost.

Writ in vacation. Court order issued during intermission of court session.

Writ of error. Appellate court orders lower court to submit record of an action on which the lower court has reached a final judgment, so that the appellate court may examine the alleged errors of the lower court.

Chapter V

BIBLIOGRAPHY

Alexander, Uhlman S. *Special Legislation Affecting Public Schools.* New York, N. Y.: Columbia University, 1929.

Allen, Ira Madison. *The Teacher's Contractual Status* (as revealed by analysis of American court decisions). New York, N. Y.: Columbia University, 1928.

Armstrong, W. Earl, and Stinnet, T. M. *A Manual on Certification for School Personnel in the United States.* Washington, D. C.: National Education Association, 1957.

Beach, Fred. *The State and Nonpublic Schools.* United States Government Publication, 1958.

Benedetti, Eugene. *School Law Materials: Cases and Materials.* Dubuque, Ia.: Wm. C. Brown, 1964.

Berman, Daniel M. *It Is So Ordered: The Supreme Court Rules on School Segregation.* New York, N.Y.: Norton, 1966.

Boles, Donald E. *The Bible, Religion and the Public Schools.* Ames, Ia.: Iowa State University Press, 1961.

Bryson, Joseph E. *Legality of Loyalty Oath and Non-Oath Requirements for Public School Teachers.* Bonne, N.C.: Appalachian State Teachers College, 1963.

Callahan, Daniel J. *Federal Aid and Catholic Schools.* Baltimore, Md.: Helicon Press, 1964.

Chambers, M. M. *The Colleges and the Courts.* Boston, Mass.: Merrymount Press, 1941.

Chambers, M. M. *The Colleges and the Courts, 1962-1966.* Danville, Ill.: The Interstate Printers & Publishers, Inc., 1967.

Chambers, M. M. *The Colleges and the Courts Since 1950.* Danville, Ill.: The Interstate Printers & Publishers, Inc., 1964.

Defending and Legally Establishing the Good News. Brooklyn, N. Y.: Watchtower Bible and Tract Society, Inc., 1950.

Douglas, William O. *The Bible and the Schools.* Boston, Mass.: Little, Brown & Co., 1966.

Drinan, Robert F. *Religion, the Courts and Public Policy.* New York, N.Y.: McGraw-Hill Book Co., Inc., 1966.

Drouin, Edward G. *The School Question.* Washington, D.C.: Catholic University of America Press, 1963.

Drury, Robert L., and others. *Law and the School Superintendent.* (The National Organization on Legal Problems of Education) Cincinnati, Ohio: W. H. Anderson, 1958.

Drury, Robert L., and Ray, Kenneth. *Principles of School Law, with Cases.* New York, N.Y.: Appleton-Century-Crofts, 1965.

Duker, Sam. *The Public Schools and Religion, the Legal Context.* New York, N.Y.: Harper and Row, 1965.

Edwards, Newton. *The Courts and the Public Schools.* Chicago, Ill.: University of Chicago, 1955.

Elliot, E. C. *Legislation upon Industrial Education in the United States.* National Society for Promotion of Industrial Education, Bulletin #12, 1910.

Fellman, David. *The Supreme Court and Education.* New York, N.Y.: Bureau of Publications, Teachers College, Columbia University Press, 1960.

Flowers, Anne, and Bolmeier, Edward C. *Law and Pupil Control.* Cincinnati, Ohio: W. H. Anderson, 1964.

Fraenkel, Osmond K. *The Supreme Court and Civil Liberties.* Dobb's Ferry, N.Y.: Oceana, 1963.

Freund, Paul A., and Ulrich, Robert. *Religion and the Public Schools.* Cambridge, Mass.: Harvard University Press, 1965.

Fulbright, Evelyn R., and Bolmeier, Edward C. *Courts and the Curriculum.* Cincinnati, Ohio: W. H. Anderson, 1964.

Garber, Lee O. *Handbook of School Law.* New London, Conn.: Arthur C. Croft Publications, 1954.

Garber, Lee O. *The Law and the Teacher in Pennsylvania.* Philadelphia: Educational Service Bureau, University of Pennsylvania, 1955.

Garber, Lee O., and Benedetti, Eugene. *The Law and the Teacher in California.* Danville, Ill.: The Interstate Printers & Publishers, Inc., 1967.

Garber, Lee O., Drury, Robert L., and Shaw, Roger M. *The Law and the Teacher in Ohio.* Danville, Ill.: The Interstate Printers & Publishers, Inc., 1966.

Garber, Lee O., and Edwards, Newton. *School Law Casebook Series,* No. 1-8. Danville, Ill.: The Interstate Printers & Publishers, Inc.

Garber, Lee O., and Hageny, William J. *The Law and the Teacher in New York State.* Danville, Ill.: The Interstate Printers & Publishers, Inc., 1967.

Garber, Lee O., and Micken, Charles M. *The Commonwealth, the Law, and the Teacher.* Danville, Ill.: The Interstate Printers & Publishers, Inc., 1963.

Garber, Lee O., and Reutter, E. Edmund, Jr. *Yearbook of School Law.* Danville, Ill.: The Interstate Printers & Publishers, Inc., published annually.

Garber, Lee O., and Smith, H. H. *The Law and the Teacher in Illinois.* Danville, Ill.: The Interstate Printers & Publishers, Inc., 1965.

Gauerke, Warren E. *Legal and Ethical Responsibilities of School Personnel.* Englewood Cliffs, N. J.: Prentice-Hall, Inc., 1959.

Gauerke, Warren E. *School Law.* Chicago, Ill.: Center for Applied Research in Education, 1965.
Griffiths, William Edward. *Religion, the Courts and the Public Schools.* Cincinnati, Ohio: W. H. Anderson, 1966.
Hamilton, Robert R. *Legal Rights and Liabilities of Teachers.* Laramie, Wyo.: School Law Publication, 1956.
Hamilton, Robert R. *The National School Law Reporter.* New London, Conn.: Arthur C. Croft Publications, Bi-weekly publication.
Hamilton, Robert, and Mort, Paul. *The Law and Public Education.* Brooklyn, N. Y.: The Foundation Press, Inc., 1959.
Hamilton, Robert, and Reutter, E. Edmund, Jr. *Legal Aspects of School Board Operation.* New York, N.Y.: Bureau of Publications, Teachers College, Columbia University Press, 1958.
Hobson, Elsie Garland. *Educational Legislation and Administration in New York from 1777 to 1850.* Chicago, Ill.: University of Chicago, 1918.
Hood, William Ross. *Digest of State Laws Relating to Public Education.* Washington, D. C.: United States Government Printing Office, 1916.
Huston, Wendell. *School Laws of the Forty-Eight States.* Seattle, Wash.: W. Huston Co., 1947.
Jacobs, Milton C. *School Law (for Teachers).* New York, N. Y.: Aberdeen Press, 1951.
James, K. F. *Corporal Punishment in the Public Schools,* Los Angeles, Calif.: University of Southern California Press, 1963.
Keesecker, Ward W. *State Boards of Education and Chief State School Officers: Their Status and Legal Powers.* Washington, D. C.: United States Government Printing Office, Office of Education, Bulletin #12, 1950.
Keesecker, Ward W., and Allen, Alfred C. *Compulsory Education Requirements.* Washington, D. C.: Department of Health, Education and Welfare, Office of Education, Circular #440, 1955.
Kigin, Denis J. *Teacher Liability in School-Shop Accidents.* Ann Arbor, Mich.: Prakken, 1963.
Legal Almanac Series (No. 17) *Education Law Simplified.* New York, N. Y.: Oceana Publications, Inc., 1959.
Leibee, Howard C. *Tort Liability for Injuries to Pupils.* Ann Arbor, Mich.: Campus Publishers, 1965.
Lieberman, Myron, and Moskow, Michael H. *Collective Negotiations for Teachers.* Chicago, Ill.: Rand McNally, 1966.
Loughery, Bernard F. *Parental Rights in American Educational Law.* Washington, D.C.: Catholic University of American Press, 1957.
Martens, Elise H. *State Legislation for Education of Exceptional Children.* United States Government Printing Office, Office of Education, Bulletin #2, 1949.
Matzen, John Mathiason. *State Constitutional Provisions for Educations.* New York, N. Y.: Columbia University Press, 1931.
McGrath, John J. *Church and State in American Law.* Milwaukee, Wisc.: Bruce, 1964.
Miller, Edward Alanson. *The History of Educational Legislation in Ohio from 1803 to 1850.* Columbus, Ohio: The Ohio State University, 1918.

Minnesota State Board of Education. *Laws of Minnesota Relating to the Public School System.* St. Paul, Minn.: Minnesota Department of Education, 1946.

Morrison, John C. *Legal Status of the City School Superintendent.* Baltimore, Md.: Warwick and York, 1922.

National Education Association, Research Division. "The Codification of School Law," *Research Bulletin,* Vol. 32, No. 1, 1954. Washington, D. C.: NEA, 1954.

National Education Association, Research Division. *High Spots in State School Legislation.* Washington, D. C.: NEA, Annual.

National Education Association, Research Division. *Legal Status of Segregated Schools.* Washington, D. C.: NEA, 1954.

National Education Association, Research Division. "The Legal Status of the Public-School Teacher," *Research Bulletin,* Vol. 25, No. 2, April, 1947. Washington, D. C.: NEA, 1947.

National Education Association, Research Division. "Legal Status of the School Superintendent," *Research Bulletin,* Vol. 29, No. 3, October, 1951. Washington, D. C.: NEA, 1951.

National Education Association, Research Division. "Public School Retirement at the Half Century," *Research Bulletin,* Vol. 27, No. 4, 1950. Washington, D. C.: NEA, 1950.

National Education Association, Research Division. *Pupils' Day in Court.* Washington, D. C.: NEA, Annual.

National Education Association, Research Division. *The School Teacher's Day in Court.* Washington, D. C.: NEA, Annual.

National Education Association, Research Division. "The State and Sectarian Education," *Research Bulletin,* Vol. 34, No. 4, December, 1956. Washington, D. C.: NEA, 1956.

National Education Association, Research Division. "State Legislation Affecting School Revenues," *Research Bulletin,* Vol. 32, No. 3, October, 1954. Washington, D. C.: NEA, 1954.

National Education Association, Research Division. *Tax Limitation Laws.* Washington, D. C.: NEA, 1956.

National Education Association, Research Division. *The Teacher and the Law.* School Law Series, Research Monograph 1959-M3. Washington, D. C.: NEA, 1959.

National Education Association, Research Division. *Who Is Liable for Pupil Injuries?* Washington, D.C.: NEA, 1963.

Nolte, Chester M., and Linn, John Phillip. *School Law for Teachers.* Danville, Ill.: The Interstate Printers & Publishers, Inc., 1963.

Nolte, Chester M., and Simpson, Robert J. *Education and the Law in Colorado.* Cincinnati, Ohio: W. H. Anderson, 1966.

Phenix, Philip H. *Education and the Worship of God.* Philadelphia: Westminister Press, 1966.

Price, Miles Oscar, and Bitner, Harry. *Effective Legal Research.* New York, N. Y.: Prentice-Hall, Inc., 1953.

Punke, Harold H. *Community Uses of Public School Facilities.* New York, N. Y.: King's Crown Press, 1951.

Punke, Harold H. *The Courts and Public School Property*. Chicago, Ill.: University of Chicago Press, 1936.

Remmlein, Madaline Kinter. *School Law*. Danville, Ill.: The Interstate Printers & Publishers, Inc., 1962.

Remmlein, Madaline Kinter. *The Law of Local Public School Administration*. New York, N. Y.: McGraw-Hill Book Co., Inc., 1953.

Remmlein, Madaline Kinter, and Ware, Martha L. *An Evaluation of Existing Forms of School Laws*. (The National Organization on Legal Problems of Education) Cincinnati, Ohio: The W. H. Anderson Co., 1959.

Reutter, E. Edmund, Jr., *Schools and the Law*. Dobb's Ferry, N.Y.: Oceana, 1960.

Rezny, Arthur A. *The Law and the School Administrator—Case Book*. Milwaukee, Wisc.: University Extension, University of Wisconsin, 1967.

Rezny, Arthur A. *Legal Problems of School Boards*. Cincinnati, Ohio: W. H. Anderson, 1966.

Rosenfield, Harry Nathan. *Liability for School Accidents, A Manual for Education Administrators and Teachers*. New York, N. Y.: Harper & Brothers, 1940.

Seitz, Reynolds C. *Law and the School Principal*. Cincinnati, Ohio: W. H. Anderson, 1961.

Simpson, Robert J. *The Educator and the Law in Hawaii*. Honolulu: University of Hawaii Press, 1964.

Singer, H. Halleck, and Micken, Charles M. *The Law of Purchasing*. Danville, Ill.: The Interstate Printers & Publishers, Inc., 1964.

Smith, James H. *Legal Limitations on Bonds and Taxation for Public School Buildings*. New York, N. Y.: Columbia University, 1930.

Smodic, William J. *The Law and After-Hours Use of School Facilities*. Pittsburgh, Pa.: M. S. Press, 1965.

Soper, Wayne W. *Legal Limitations of the Rights and Powers of School Boards in Respect to Taxation*. New York, N. Y.: Columbia University, 1929.

Spurlock, Clark. *Education and the Supreme Court*. Champaign, Ill.: University of Illinois Press, 1955.

State School Laws, and Regulations for Health, Safety, Driver, Outdoor and Physical Education. Washington, D.C.: United States Government Printing Office, 1964.

Steiner, Arch K. "A Report on State Laws: Early Elementary Education," *School Life*, Vol. 39, May, 1957.

Summaries of Rulings of State Attorneys General with Respect to Church-State Questions as They Affect Public and Parochial Schools. Compiled by The American Jewish Committee, 386 Fourth Avenue, New York 16, N. Y., and Anti-Defamation League of B'nai B'rith, 515 Madison Avenue, New York 22, N. Y., 1958.

Swalls, Fred. *Legal Aspects of Student Teaching*. Danville, Ill.: The Interstate Printers & Publishers, Inc., 1966.

Symposium on School Law. *Current Legal Concepts in Education*. Philadelphia: University of Pennsylvania Press, 1966.

Taylor, Marvin J. *Religious and Moral Education.* Chicago, Ill.: Center for Applied Research in Education, 1965.

Trusler, Harry Raymond. *Essentials of School Law.* Milwaukee, Wis.: The Bruce Publishing Co., 1927.

Tussman, Joseph. *The Supreme Court on Church and State.* New York, N.Y.: Oxford University Press, 1962.

Tussman, Joseph. *The Supreme Court on Racial Discrimination.* New York, N.Y.: Oxford University Press, 1963.

United States Bureau of Education. *Compulsory School Attendance.* Washington, D. C.: United States Government Printing Office, 1914.

United States Bureau of Education. *Legislative and Judicial Decisions Relative to Education.* Washington, D. C.: United States Government Printing Office, 1909 (also 1910 and 1913).

United States Department of Health, Education and Welfare, Office of Education. *Federal Laws and Rulings Relating to Morrill and Supplementary Morrill Funds for Land-Grant Colleges and Universities.* Pamphlet No. 91, 1940.

United States Department of Health, Education and Welfare, Office of Education. *School Transportation Insurance, Legal Bases and Current Practice.* Pamphlet No. 101, United States Government Printing Office, 1948.

Voorhees, Harvey Cortlandt. *The Law of the Public School System of the United States.* Boston, Mass.: Little, Brown & Co., 1916.

Ware, Martha. *Law of Guidance and Counseling.* Cincinnati, Ohio: W. H. Anderson, 1964.

Weathersby, William Henington. *A History of Educational Legislation in Mississippi from 1798 to 1860.* Chicago, Ill.: University of Chicago, 1921.

Wisconsin State Superintendent's Office. *Laws of Wisconsin Relating to Public Schools.* Madison, Wis.: Democrat Printing Company, various years since 1885. Also School Law Supplement.

Yakel, Ralph. *The Legal Control of the Administration of Public School Expenditures.* New York, N. Y.: Columbia University, 1929.

NOTES

NOTES

NOTES

NOTES